A Pre-Primer
for
Beginners
in
Genealogical Search

What to Read
before
Your First How-To Book

Sophie C. Fisher, M.A.

HERITAGE BOOKS
2010

HERITAGE BOOKS

AN IMPRINT OF HERITAGE BOOKS, INC.

Books, CDs, and more—Worldwide

For our listing of thousands of titles see our website
at
www.HeritageBooks.com

Published 2010 by
HERITAGE BOOKS, INC.
Publishing Division
100 Railroad Ave. #104
Westminster, Maryland 21157

International Standard Book Numbers
Paperbound: 978-0-7884-5269-7
Clothbound: 978-0-7884-8587-9

CONTENTS

LIST OF ILLUSTRATIONS

PREFACE

This is a pre-primer for someone who decided to look into genealogy and knows absolutely nothing about it.

Which is how I started.

This book is for the absolute beginner, to get organized as you start your genealogical research--not after you have accumulated years of clippings, vital records, correspondence, census figures, etc. that managed to get jumbled up on your desk or table, or in your files or other places.

You've come across an old letter, found an old photo or overheard someone talking about how they traced their family back several generations. This piqued your interest and you wondered how to go about tracing your own family line back.

Or, perhaps a family member left you all his or her genealogical papers and you would like to continue research.

How far back can you go? Where did your family start? In what county, state, country did they first appear? Where did your family name originate. Who were your forebears? What did they look like? Where did they live? What did they do? Was their life hard or easy? Were they healthy? What did they pass down to you--their looks, their genes, their talents? What is their story? This will be part of your story.

When I decided it might be a good idea to put together a family genealogy to save my family's history, I had no idea of what to do first.

I want to include items based on my trial-and-error, time-consuming experience where I wasted much time redoing things as long as seven years after I started. I back-tracked, lost records, duplicated work, and got bogged down, because I didn't know about some procedures. I want to show how I simplified my methods from the ones I used at first.

I'd like to cover how to collect data on yourself and your relatives, where to keep it, places you can find it, how to write to try to find more, how to organize it, document it and get it all together. We could call it data-collecting methodology with a provable result.

The long-term goal is to put your information into a family history or genealogical form, one generation after the other, researched and documented, so that the results of your research and the history of your family are available to all the descendants of this particular family, which is probably spread far and wide, with some unaware of how far back their heritage goes.

An important note: keep track of your expenses from the beginning. Get a ledger book and list books purchased, postage on letters sent, cost of equipment, paper, supplies and money spent of having research done. At some point in time, this is information you will need.

As you become familiar with the procedures of genealogy, you will soon be or are now aware of new technical developments for information: personal computers, data bases on CD-ROMs, genealogical software, the Internet, E-Mail, etc. However, before you get involved with these, you still have to accumulate information to work with and establish a base. Then you can venture into computerized data. What you find can then be added to what you have.

I hope this pre-primer will simplify your beginning research and get you started right away.

* * * * *

I got interested in genealogy by a chance reading of a notice
in the local paper of a meeting held at the Public Library by
the Genealogical Society, open to the public.

I had become curious about exactly what genealogy was all
about, especially since it was soon after Roots by Alex Haley
became popular and there was a flurry of interest in tracing
one's forebears.

I went by myself at 8:00 pm and saw the room was filled with
people I had never seen before. Tables were set up at the back
with books and leaflets for sale and I looked through them,
though they were meaningless to me at that time.

I sat at the back of the room. The topic was rubbings on
cemetary stones. And how to find the cemetaries. And how to
get death certificates. And how to fill out five-generation
pedigree sheets.

I was so fascinated that I resolved to get started right away
tracing my husband's family. When the meeting was over, I
bought some pedigree sheets. The speaker said that was the
place to start.

When I got home, I tried to fill out the pedigree sheets. They
are a chart of your forebears staring with yourself or the
person whose line you will follow, going backwards in time.

I put down my husband, his mother and father and his father's
father. That was all I knew. But what next? His mother and
father were quite elderly. Time was of the essence to get as
much information from them as we could. (This is usually where
one says, "Why didn't I start 30 years ago?") So I wrote to
them and got the little they remembered. But then again, what
next? And how do I go about it?

I joined the Genealogical Society, went to meetings and
genealogical classes.

I learned what books were recommended, which ones were in the Genealogy Room at the library and which ones to send away for. I sent for some; read others at the library. But the majority were too advanced for me. It was not easy to find how one went on after the first relatives were input.

I spent many years trying to figure what to do and how to store my records, etc. Only after culling bits and pieces from all those books, genealogical meetings, and classes did I get started in the right direction. After 10 years of seeking, a correspondence course with the National Genealogical Society gave me a lot of answers.

What chaos there was when I first began accumulating information. Some books said use manila folders; I did, but that became unwieldy for all the material I had. Others said put everything in a book with divider tabs. That became increasingly bulky; especially when I didn't want to put the originals in the books. I copied them and put the copies in the book. Originals grew to so many and so many sizes and shapes, I started to use a box.

It got completely out of hand with scraps of papers, folders and books everywhere. I couldn't find anything right away.

I finally used manila folders for each person; notebooks for each family; a 8 x 14 3-ring binder with archival vinyl sheet protectors sealed on three sides, open at the top, for vital records and another book for original wills, probates and deeds.

And I learned more efficient research methods.

I cannot believe I did so many things over, and still do, but less, before I learned simpler methods. Why hadn't I heard about all these research aids sooner? This is what I'd like to convey to you in a plain manner.

Anyway, I learned how to get death certificates, I finally found some of the cemeteries, but I have never begun to get rubbings on cemetery stones.

ABBREVIATIONS

These are some abbreviations that genealogists use:

ab.	about
aft.	after
bap.	baptized
bef.	before
b.p.	birthplace
b.	born
bur.	buried
ca.	circa (about)
cem.	cemetery
Co.	county
dau.	daughter
d.p.	death place
d.	died
d.y.	died young
m.	married
N.D.	no date
N.p.	no place
N.pub.	No publisher
p.,pp	page, pages
rpt.	reprint
res.	resided
rev.	revised
twp.	township
vol.	volume

CHAPTER 1

YOU AND YOUR FAMILY

1. Write down all you know about yourself. This is the basic starting point in all books about research in genealogy.

2. Write down all you know about your father, mother, siblings, grandparents, great-grandparents, as far back as you can go.

3. List in a column all the names of your relatives you have ever heard of.

4. Check out family bibles, documents and memorabilia.

5. Gather as much information you can from your relatives.

6. Evaluate and analyze all information to see if it is probable. Be aware errors were made in transcribing data.

7. Obtain copies of five-generation pedigree charts and family group sheets from the Genealogy Room at your library. Or use a plain piece of paper until you get these documents and draw your own. Later, you can purchase these.

Data on You and Your Family

Write down all you know about yourself and your father, mother, grandparents, etc. Add each person's birth date, marriage date, their father and mother, and in some cases, the death date. This is the information you will use to trace your family back from the present.

List in a column all your aunts, uncles, cousins, great-aunts and uncles, in-laws--everyone you can remember. Some people have a lot of relatives who can remember a lot and some have very few who can't remember anything.

Fig. 1.

PEDIGREE CHART

Compiler _Sophie C. Fisher_

The first person on this chart is the same
person as No. _8_ on chart No. _1_

CHART NO. (2)

Address _____

Date _____

KEY:
ca. about
cont. continuation
b. date of birth
p.b. place of birth
m. date of marriage
p.m. place of marriage
d. date of death
p.d. place of death
Record dates as day, month, year:
4 July 1776
Record places as city (county) state
Chicago (Cook) Illinois

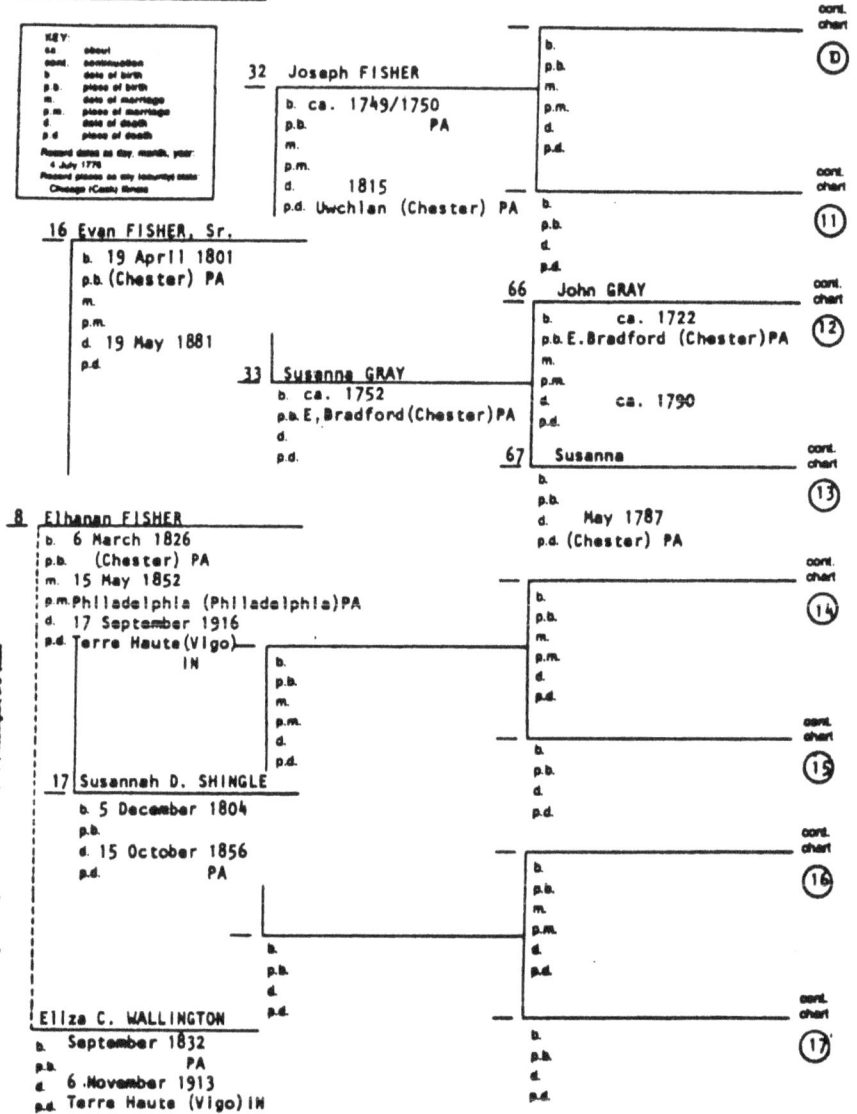

32 Joseph FISHER
b. ca. 1749/1750
p.b.   PA
m.
p.m.
d.   1815
p.d. Uwchlan (Chester) PA

16 Evan FISHER, Sr.
b. 19 April 1801
p.b. (Chester) PA
m.
p.m.
d. 19 May 1881
p.d.

33 Susanna GRAY
b. ca. 1752
p.b. E. Bradford (Chester) PA
d.
p.d.

8 Elhanan FISHER
b. 6 March 1826
p.b. (Chester) PA
m. 15 May 1852
p.m. Philadelphia (Philadelphia) PA
d. 17 September 1916
p.d. Terre Haute (Vigo) IN

17 Susannah D. SHINGLE
b. 5 December 1804
p.b.
d. 15 October 1856
p.d.   PA

Eliza C. WALLINGTON
b.   September 1832
p.b.   PA
d. 6 November 1913
p.d. Terre Haute (Vigo) IN

b.
p.b.
m.
p.m.
d.
p.d.

cont. chart (10)

b.
p.b.
d.
p.d.

cont. chart (11)

66 John GRAY
b.   ca. 1722
p.b. E. Bradford (Chester) PA
m.
p.m.
d.   ca. 1790
p.d.

cont. chart (12)

67 Susanna
b.
p.b.
d.   May 1787
p.d. (Chester) PA

cont. chart (13)

b.
p.b.
m.
p.m.
d.
p.d.

cont. chart (14)

b.
p.b.
d.
p.d.

cont. chart (15)

b.
p.b.
m.
p.m.
d.
p.d.

cont. chart (16)

b.
p.b.
d.
p.d.

cont. chart (17)

b.
p.b.
m.
p.m.
d.
p.d.

b.
p.b.
d.
p.d.

National Genealogical Society, 1921 Sunderland Pl. N.W., Washington, D.C. 20036

2

YOU AND YOUR FAMILY

Look for family bibles, legal papers, deeds, school and work records, certificates, old diaries, letters, news clippings, awards, photograph albums, etc. Be aware of variations in spelling of names in the early days and use of nicknames. Sometimes, first or last names were changed.

How To Prepare a Five-Generation Pedigree Chart

A pedigree chart is a document on which you start with yourself and work backward toward previous generations, starting with your mother and father, each of their mothers and fathers, and so on, back in time. (See Fig. 1.)

Under each name are spaces for birthdate, birthplace, death, deathplace, marriage. They are abbreviated: b.,bp.,d.,dp.,m.

1. Put your full name on Line 1, first name, middle name and capitalized last name. If you are female, use maiden name.

2. Fill in your date and place of birth. Write the date with the day, month and year: 24 August 1997 or 24 Aug 1997. Be consistent; use one of these forms for all your records. Don't write the month first or use a number for the month.

   Write the place with city, county and state, with the postal abbreviation for state, such as, Flint, Genesee Co., MI. Use Co. for county. You need to know the county; records are usually by county.

3. If married, record date and place. Write spouse's name at bottom in provided space.

4. Fill in your father's name on Line 2 and mother's maiden name on Line 3. Your father's father will be 4 and his mother will be 5. Your mother's father will be number 6 and her mother will be number 7, etc. Even numbers are used for males and uneven numbers for females.

5. Fill in all the information you have so far on birthdates, etc. for all the people you put on your pedigree chart.

6. Go back as many generations as you can, but don't skip generations.

7. On the right-hand side of the chart, enter numbers showing on which chart data on that person is continued.

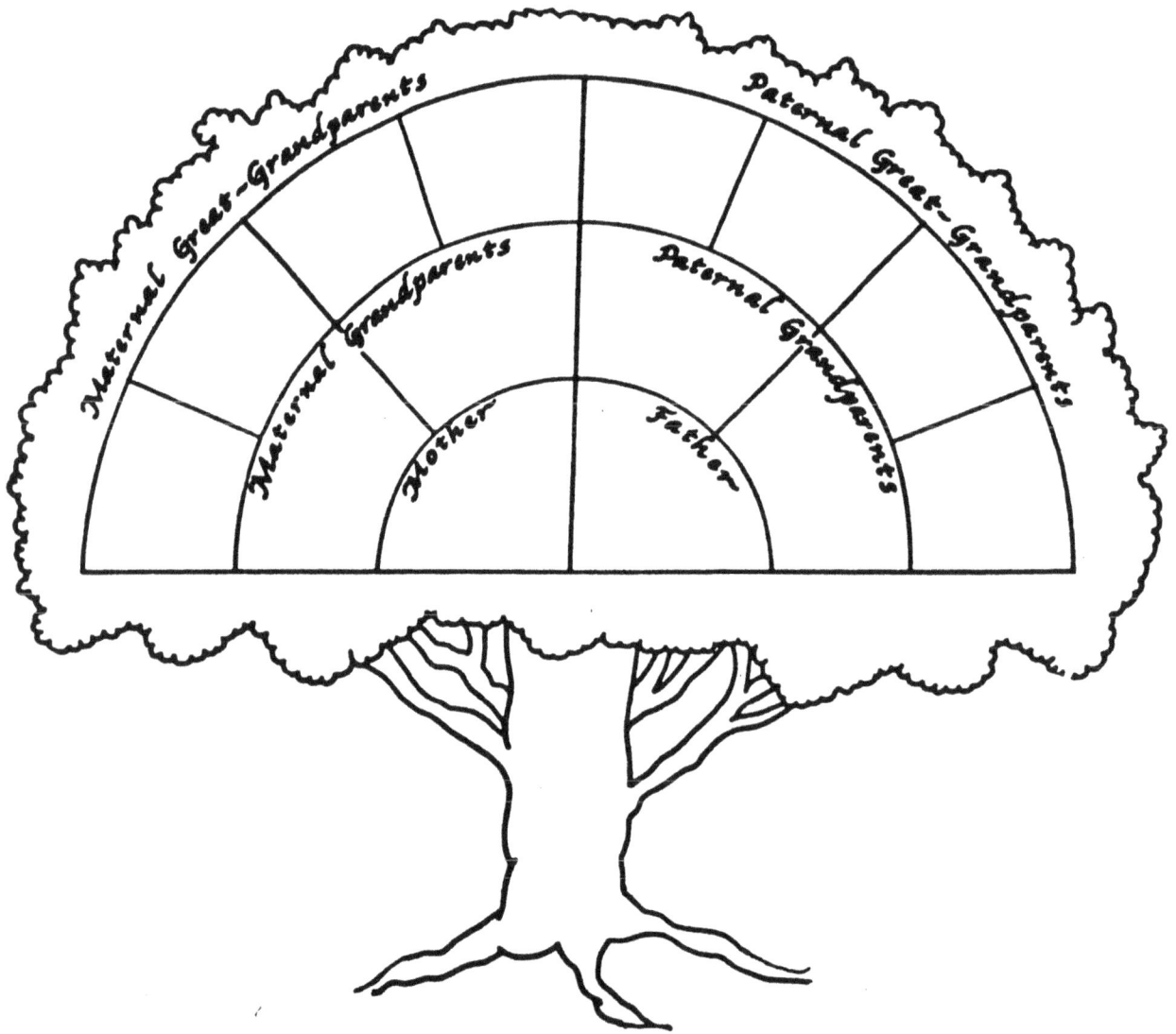

YOU AND YOUR FAMILY

As noted, you can purchase pedigree charts and family group sheets on acid-free paper from a genealogical society, usually listed in the phone book, or from companies who sell genealogical supplies. You can also find them on sale from vendors at genealogical seminars.

You can purchase large family tree charts, many beautifully illustrated, on which to input your pedigree, from many companies advertising in the genealogical publications.

Source of Documentation

From the beginning, document sources on the bottom or the back of the chart. Write this information using numbers given to each person on the chart. Some charts have a different arrangement of where to put documentation.

Show where and when you got the original or copies of birth, marriage or death certificates or other records: courthouse, government offices, health departments or other. Put down volume and page number, the number of the certificate, who you talked to or wrote to, where family bibles are located from which you got information--any information that would be helpful in finding it again by you or someone else. (Also, see Chapter 7 Documenting Your Information.)

In family bibles, note the publication date and if entries had earlier dates. If so, they could have been copied and errors could have been made. Try to verify these dates and note this in your citing. Note in whose possession the bible is.

Evaluate the information to see if it is probable. Check out conflicting data. Just because someone sent you the information doesn't mean it is right. If it is documented, you should go to the source to doublecheck it; it could have been transcribed wrongly. If you are not sure, use a question mark or state you haven't been able to verify the data.

Calendar Changes and Quaker Dates

In 1752, in the English colonies and England, the calendar was changed from Julian to Gregorian. The start of the year was moved from 25 March to the previous 1 January.

Fig. 2.

Family Group Sheet

Husband's Full Name FISHER, Elhanan   Chart No.

	Day Month Year	City, Town or Place	County or Province, etc.	State or Country	Add Info on Husb
Birth	6 Mar 1826		Chester	PA	
Chr'nd					
Marr	15 May 1852	W. Philadelphia	Philadelphia	PA	
Death	17 Sep 1916	Terre Haute	Vigo	IN	
Burial		Mt. Carroll Oak Hill Cem.	Carroll	IL	

Places of Residence PA, IL, IND.
Occupation Teacher, Shoemaker   Church Affiliation   Military Rec Civil War IL Inf 146th Co. A. GAR
His Father FISHER, Evan Sr.   Mother's Maiden Name SHINGLE, Susannah

Wife's Full Maiden Name WALLINGTON, Eliza Chamberlain

	Day Month Year	City, Town or Place	County or Province, etc.	State or Country	Add Info on Wife
Birth	Sep 1832			PA	
Chr'nd					
Death	6 Nov 1913	Terre Haute	Vigo	IN	
Burial		Mt. Carroll Oak Hill Cem.	Carroll	IL	

Places of Residence
Occupation   Church Affiliation   Military Rec.
Her Father   Mother's Maiden Name

Sex	Name		Day Month Year	City, Town or Place	County or Province, etc.	State or Country	Add Info on Ch
M	1 Edgar E. Fisher	Birth	5 Mar 1854			PA	
		Marr					
	Full Name of Spouse	Death	19 Jul 1872	Mt. Carroll	Carroll	IL	18yr, 4mo, 14d.
		Burial		Mt. Carroll	Carroll	IL	Oak Hill Cem.
F	2 Lydia Malcolm Fisher	Birth	6 Nov 1857				
		Marr					
	Full Name of Spouse	Death	23 Jan 1858	Mt. Carroll	Carroll	IL	1yr, 2mo, 17d.
		Burial		Oak Hill Cemetery	Mt. Carroll IL		Lot 39
M	3 Harvey Dunster Fisher	Birth	10 Dec 1858	Mt. Carroll	Carroll	IL	
		Marr	28 May 1881	St. Louis (City of St.Louis)		MO	
	Full Name of Spouse	Death	9 Jan 1899	Iron Mountain	Dickenson	MI	
		Burial		Quinnesec Cem.	Dickenson	MI	
M	4 Howard Malcolm Fisher	Birth	19 Oct 1861	Mt. Carroll	Carroll	IL	
		Marr	14 Dec 1882	Mt. Carroll	Carroll	IL	2nd marr. 1891
	Full Name of Spouse 1.Elsie Croom 2. Sarah	Death					
		Burial					
M	5 Robert Bell Fisher	Birth	21 Nov 1863	Mt. Carroll	Carroll	IL	
		Marr	6 Apr 1896	Perth Amboy	Middlesex	N.J	
	Full Name of Spouse Marian Parsons Roberts	Death	10 Dec 1918	Springfield	Hampden	MASS	
		Burial		Springfield			
F	6 Margaret A. Fisher	Birth	23 Feb 1867	Mt. Carroll	Carroll	IL	
		Marr	4 Sep 1894	Mt. Carroll	Carroll	IL	
	Full Name of Spouse William T. Turman	Death	12 Apr 1943	Terre Haute	Vigo	IN	
		Burial		Roselawn Memorial Park, Terre Haute,		IN	
	7	Birth					
		Marr					
	Full Name of Spouse	Death					
		Burial					
	8	Birth					
		Marr					
	Full Name of Spouse	Death					
		Burial					

Compiler Sophie Fisher   Notes
Address 5423 S. Dyewood Dr.
City, State, Zip Flint, MI 48532-3328
Date

6

Before 1752, 25 March was considered the first day of the year. Dates before 1752 for the months between 1 January and 24 March were double-dated, like 3 February 1713/1714, to avoid confusion. Before 1 January, and after 25 March, only single dates were used for each month, like 26 March 1714.

As you go back in time, if you have Quaker dates, you will find they did not use the months' names because most of them were based on names of pagan gods, but called them 1st month, 2nd month and so on.

Some researchers transcribe the Quaker dates before 1752 without using their system of 1st month, etc. or incorporating the calendar change at 1752, calling 3 12th month 1713/1714 (3 February) as 3 December 1714, which would be an incorrect date. I think it's best to leave Quaker dates with their denotation of 1st month, etc. because if they are changed into named months, one can't tell which month is meant. A Quaker date written 13 1st month, would not be 13 January, but 13 March.

The Family Group Sheet

The Family Group Sheet is prepared for each head of the family, spouse, and children in order of birth. (See Fig. 2.)

1. Fill in a Family Group Sheet for each person on the pedigree chart and his or her family: Husband and wife, their children and the data you found.

2. Fill in when and where they were born and married, died and buried. Use the notation "died young" or "d.y." for very early deaths of children; note where they died and were buried.

3. If known, for both husband and wife, enter other places lived, occupation, religion, military service, other spouses, and mother and father.

4. If the head of the family or spouse was married more than once, prepare a separate sheet for each marriage and children.

5. As you find records for them, you can document them on the sheet, as noted above for the pedigree chart.

7

The Rest of Your Family

Converse with your relatives and gather what information they can remember and would like to share, especially the older relatives.

Do they remember their mother's maiden name, their father's mother's maiden name, their first names, where they were born, went to school, married. Do they recall any other relatives?

Do they recall any places where they lived? Any special events? Do they have family bibles, documents or mementos, any announcements, news clippings, write-ups in local histories? Were there any traditions or legends in their families?

You can call or write and ask them questions. Be very specific. "Do you remember where cousin John was born? When did he come to Illinois?" "Where did you live when you went to the third grade?" You can also use a tape recorder.

You can now start pedigree charts and family group sheets for them.

Tradition or Legend

A tradition is the handing down of unwritten information by word of mouth from one generation to another; a legend is a story coming down from the past regarded as historical, but not verifiable. Our older relatives must know a lot of stories handed down from their relatives.

It's very interesting to try to discover how these traditions or legends started. You have to trace back from what you know, looking for even little clues.

If you come across any awkward information that may embarrass someone, it's up to you if you want to use it. I decided not to include anything like that in my family history.

Be prepared to use any information you receive as documentation for your genealogy. You can write, "per Cousin Mary or from John's family bible," especially if you are not able to get any other documented information.

Photographs

As you communicate with your relatives, try to accumulate as many photographs as you can from them, especially of older family members. It is very interesting to other family members to see what their ancestors looked like.

Identify all photographs with name or names, place and date taken. Do not write on the back of them with heavy ink. The best way is to type or write on a piece of self-adhesive tape, like labels, and attach to the back of the photos.

Find out if there are any stories about these photographs; on what occasion were these people photographed there? Was it in the city where they lived or had they traveled a long way to the photographic studio? There weren't any snapshots in the olden days so people had to pose quite a while for the photographer.

Clothes the subjects are wearing may approximate the time period if none is known.

If photographs are very old, make copies of them in black and white to safeguard them. I've had photographs, which were taken in the late 1800's and mounted on cardboard, break in half. The edges crumble and fall off. If exposed to light, they may fade.

Laser computer copies and restoration services are becoming more common and easier to find. Some one-hour photo shops send away photographs to be restored after making a copy of them. They also make laser copies.

Previously, before computer restoration, I sent away an original photograph to be restored. It took three months and in transit back to me, a part of the original broke off. New procedures are: you keep the original and the copy is sent.

Archival supplies are available for safe storage of photographs, both boxes and albums. Don't use plain cardboard boxes as they will damage your photos. Also don't use the old albums which have magnetic clear pages that go over the photos which attach to the page. Albums are available that hold the photos in by black or clear corners on acid-free pages and preserve them for a long time.

You can get these from companies that make archival supplies and advertise in genealogical magazines. Some of these items are available in large office supply stores.

Now that you have something to work with, you are ready to assemble the materials to accommodate your research.

To Sum Up:

1. Collect all information you know on yourself and your family. Be aware of the various spellings of names in early days and use of nicknames. Sometimes first and last names were changed.

2. Write it all down in orderly fashion by family.

3. See family bibles, old papers, legal documents, memorabilia, etc.

4. Evaluate and analyze evidence to see if it is probable. Check out conflicting data. Be aware that many errors were made in transcription of data.

5. Prepare a five-generation pedigree chart and family group sheet for each head of family.

6. Go back as many generations as you can, but don't skip generations.

7. Enter documentation for each fact on the bottom or back of the pedigree charts and family group sheets, or elsewhere on them, stating where and when you obtained information.

8. Be aware of the calendar change in 1752 and the Quaker way of writing dates.

9. Gather photographs from as far back as you can; label each with name or names, place and date taken. Copy older photographs or restore them if damaged. Include known stories about these photographs.

10. You may want to start entering information on a large family tree.

CHAPTER 2

WHERE TO KEEP YOUR RECORDS

As you accumulate data and documents to back up your pedigree and family group sheets, you will want to prepare a place to put them all. Here is a system I used.

Gather together:

1. Manila Folders
2. Yellow Tab Dividers
3. Three-Ring Binders
4. Archival Sheet Protectors
5. Note Pad or Steno Pad
6. 3 x 5 cards
7. Plain Paper for Log Sheets
8. A Ledger to keep track of expenses--for future use.

Manila Folders

Label your manila folders with the family names you found, last name first, capitalized. Put the information you found on each person in the manila folder for him or her. Keep in a file or a box. Later, you might want to subdivide them by children, each one in a separate folder, with their families.

I started with the oldest ancestor found, keeping his children's charts in the same folder; thcn, after him, in the next folder, I put the one of his children we were following, with his family, continuing all the way back to the present person we were following.

Tab Dividers

Label your tab dividers the same way. Put them in a binder or binders. I started with my husband's family and had a binder for his mother's family and one for his father's family, starting each with the oldest known ancestor.

Binders

I used three-ring binders of various sizes--1", 2" and 3". As my material grew, I moved from smaller to larger binders.

Put your five-generation pedigree chart at the beginning of the binder or binders and family group sheets behind each tab divider. I kept the family group sheets in archival 8 1/2" x 11" sheet binders so they wouldn't become tattered and could be copied right through the clear sheets.

Later, you can make family group sheets for each of the children in the same family group. It is worthwhile to follow all the children, but I first followed the direct line down.

As you find new names, you can add more binders.

Search Document

As you start to accumulate data, insert a plain piece of paper at the beginning of each section of the binder for each family and title it SEARCH. You can also insert the SEARCH paper at the front of each manila folder.

This is to keep a record of your research on that person and family: a running tab on correspondence, list of maps where they lived, census records ordered, documents sent for--dated and itemized. Getting it all on paper will give you a good perspective on how the research is going.

Documents

At first, I kept original documents and copies and certified copies of them (which you can get at the courthouse) in the binders with the pedigree sheets and family group charts, but found that it was easier to keep them separately by family in a 8 1/2 x14 notebook in archival vinyl sheet protectors. I kept the documents by date, with the earliest date first. This makes the them easier to find than by name because you will be looking in the right time frame.

Deeds and indentures and other documents, such as wills, are usually on legal-sized paper. The copies made from the originals at the courthouse or from microfilm are also on legal-sized paper, 8 1/2" x 14", and fit in the longer sheet protectors. Nowadays, many documents are on regular paper 8 1/2" x 11.

Archival Sheet Protectors

For documents and copies of documents you will find, obtain archival clear sheet protectors and a separate binder to keep them in. Something in the composition of regular plastic sheet protectors is damaging to paper documents; that is why genealogists use archival clear ones which are considered safe. They come in 8 1/2" x 11" and 8 1/2" x 14" sizes. There are 8 1/2" x 14" three-ring binders also. Large office supply stores usually carry these.

Simplifying Storage

After a period of time, I kept only family group sheets in the binders, original documents and copies in separate binders and kept letters, news clippings, etc. in the folders with the surnames.

Other Material

As you divide the information more specifically, you can add folders for maps, land records, libraries, etc.

I kept folders for the states where ancestors lived and where we did research, but finally put this information in the folders with the ancestors it applied to.

I did maintain folders for genealogical societies and archives, mainly their location, hours and procedures. This was to obtain information, such as, at the Maryland State Archives, you can write or call to request they charge your credit card for any costs incurred and you get the information so much quicker.

I also kept a folder with how-to clippings and information.

Fig. 3. Bibliography - Publications Looked At.

```
KENTUCKY
FLINT LIBR.    LOOKED AT MUEHLENBURG CO. MARRIAGES BY COX, E 1802-1836 -NIL
               HOPKINS CO. RECORDS, VOL IV,V
               HOPKINS DEED BOOKS, I,11  - ALL NIL
               KENTUCKY MARRIAGES BY CLIFT
               KENTUCKY BIBLE RECORDS DAV VOL IV  ALL NIL
               KENTUCKY OBITS 1787-1854
               KENTUCKY - A HISTORY OF THE STATE-1887
11-13-87       EARLY KENTUCKY WILLS 1798-1824      - NIL
               THE KENTUCKY LAND GRANTS 1782-1914 - NIL
               1ST CENSUS OF KENTUCKY - 1790
               1810 KENTUCKY CENSUS - NIL
               1820 KENTUCKY CENSUS - ONLY JOHN RISTON
               1830 KENTUCKY CENSUS - ONLY JOHN WRISTON
               SURNAME INDEX TO 1850 CENSUS KENTUCKY -
               KENTUCKY MARRIAGE RECORDS - NIL
               KENTUCKY PIONEERS & THEIR DESCENDANTS-ILA EARL FOWLER
               FOR THE KENTUCKY SOCIETY DAUGHTERS OF COLONIAL WARS-BALTIMORE
               GEN. PUB CO. 1967. P.295-MARRIAGE RECORDS?
               OCT 25,1831 - WM. RISDON TO ELEN FULKS, JAS. MORSE

5-29-88        HOPKINS CO.LIBRARY. MADISONVILLE. KY GEN.SOC.PO BOX 51, 42431
               KY H 196 HOPKINS CO. KY MARRIAGES 1807-1868
                  ELIJAH WUTSON (WRISTON) & LEONA SISK OCT 11, 1832
                  REUBEN WRISTON & VERNETTA ADKINS - OCT 19, 1837
               SOME EARLY PIONEERS OF WESTERN KY, THEIR ANCESTORS & DESC. BY
               HELEN E HART PEYTON - RE: DANIEL H SISK,
               PP.418,421,333-335,411,412,416-417 (HE SOLD LAND TO ELIJAH
               RISTON AND THEN WENT OUT TO PARKER COUNTY, TEXAS WITH HIS
               FAMILY)
               PENSION ABSTRACTS-CHRISTIAN CO. JOSEPH WRISTON, MAJOR ?

               KY C 112 MARRIAGE RECORDS 1797-1850,1851-1900 (KY C 113)
               CHRISTIAN CO. KY
               1.  HENRIETTA WRISTON-COLEMAN DAVIS   1823
               2.  MARTHA WRISTON-ANDREW REDD        1835
               3.  POLLY WRISTON-JESSE HARDISON      1840

               CHRISTIAN CO. KY 1850 FED CENSUS
                  787-835 NANCY WRISTON   79 F   W   B. 1771  MD
                          ELIZT           50 F   W   B. 1800  VA
                          JOS             21 M   W   B. 1829  KY
                  COULD HE BE THE MAJOR FOR WHOM THERE WERE PENSION ABSTR.? GJt
                  629-672 HENRIETTA DAVIS 57 F   W   B. 1793  VA
                          MARTIN C        21 M   W   B. 1829  KY FARMER
                          WADE H          18 M   W   B. 1832  KY TEACHER
                          LEANDER R.      16 M   W   B. 1834  KY
                          GEORGEL.NEWCOMB 13 M   W   B. 1837  KY
                          SARAH A WRISTON 80 F   W            MD

               KY H 187 CHRISTIAN CO. KY 1860 FED CENSUS
                  465/465 WRISTON, JAMES  M   30    B. 1830  KY
                          E.Elizabeth ?   F   63    B. 1797  VA

               KY H 189 CHRISTIAN CO KY 1880 FED CENSUS - NO WRISTONS
               CHRISTIAN CO KY 1810 FED CENSUS - NO WRISTONS
```

14

WHERE TO KEEP YOUR RECORDS

Steno Pad or Small Notebook

When you take the steno pad or small notebook with you to keep track of your research, be sure to put down the date you are using it and where.

3x5 Cards

Some people prepare 3x5 cards with name, date of birth, marriage, spouse, their dates of birth and death, parents of both, and place and date of death for each ancestor, but I didn't. I found the binders and manila folders were enough to begin with, but you may prefer cards.

Preparation of Log Sheets

Get four sheets of plain paper to prepare logs. Head them:

    BIBLIOGRAPHY
    CORRESPONDENCE LOG
    DIARY
    CENSUSES ORDERED OR USED

These can be kept in one or more binders.

Bibliography

Keeping a bibliography (See Fig. 3.) is very important. Unless you write down the title and author for every book you take down from the shelf and glance at, you will be back at the library, going thru all of the same books again, saying, this looks familiar; why didn't I note it down the first time?

If you go to more than one library, you may find yourself taking notes from one book, going home, and finding you had taken notes from that book at another library. Worse, is looking in a book and finding nothing and going home and see you saw that before and had forgotten.

From the beginning, write down title and author of each book you look at and at which library seen. Write down publisher, date and place printed on those with information you can use. Make a copy of the title page if possible, to make it easier later for documentation. Since I didn't do this at first, I had to go back to the library and look up these books again.

Fig. 4. Correspondence Log.

CORRESPONDENCE RECORD

	DATE SENT	ADDRESSEE/ADDRESS	PURPOSE	DATE REPLIED	COST	RESULTS
1.	4-12-82	Iowa Dept of Health	Birth Cert. R. W. Fisher, Jr.	4-15-82	2	YES
2.	4-14-82	Co. Clerk, Dickenson Co. Michigan	Death Cert. H. D. Fisher	4-20-82	10	YES
3.	4-28-82	Illinois Dept of Health H. D. Fisher	Birth Cert. H. D. Fisher	X	3	NIL
4.	4-28-82	Missouri Dept of Health	Birth Cert. H. D. Fisher	X	1	NIL
5.	4-28-82	Texas Dept of Health	Birth Cert. H. D. Fisher	X	5	NIL
6.	5-10-82	Mt. Carroll Co. Clk Mt. Carroll, MI	Marriage Cert H. D. Fisher	X	3 / 3	NIL / NIL
7.	5-17-82	Taylor Co. Clk	Marriage Cert	X	3	NIL
8.	5-17-82	Callahan Co. Tx	Death Cert. W. H. Wristen	5-24-82	3	YES no probate available
9.	5-17-82	Taylor Co. Tx.	Birth Cert. W. H. Wristen	X	3	NIL
10.	5-17-82	Jefferson Co.	Birth Cert. W. H. Wristen	X	3	NIL
11.	5-17-82	El Paso, Tex	Death Cert Emma Rose Knight	X	5	NIL
12.	5-17-82	St. Louis Co.	Birth & Death Cert. Katie Spears Fisher	X	2	NIL
13.	5-17-82	Birmingham, Ala.	Birth Cert. Emma Rose Knight	X	NC	NIL

16

Make a list of books seen and take it to the library when you go. I now list books I read by state, showing what library I found them in, and include a little summary of content.

Correspondence Log

A correspondence log (See Fig. 4.) is important too. From the beginning you will write letters and get answers. First you will probably file the letters with the person referred to, but soon your correspondence will become too bulky to handle or too hard to find, as you write letters to county clerks, genealogical societies, state libraries and various other places you never dreamed of.

It's easiest to make up a correspondence log right away before you send your first letter.

Draw some lines across and down to make columns. Head them:

No.	Date Sent	Addressee/ Address	Purpose	Date Replied	Cost	Results

Put the log in a binder. Number copies of letters sent. Enter their number in the log and keep them in the same book. You may not wish to make copies; just write a summary on your log.

It is considered polite to send self-addressed stamped envelopes with your letters of inquiry. However, once I sent out 40 letters with SASEs to individuals and only received three replies. This becomes expensive. In the long run, though, this is the most possible way to get a reply.

As you get answers, either make a note on your letter that was answered or put the reply behind the letter in the book. Or make a notation on the logsheet next to your summary, using the same number. Reference the number of other correspondence from that person or organization. Also, note the receipt of all documents by mail on your log.

After a while, I decided to put only pertinent letters in the logbook--those with positive responses which would advance the research. The negative responses, I just noted on the log.

Fig. 5. Census Log.

NAME	DATE	YEAR	STATE	COUNTY	SOUNDEX NO.	REEL	SOUNDEX NAME	FILM VOL.	REEL	PAGE	E.D.	SHEET/LINE	TOWN	REC'D
FISHER, ELIJAH	3/6	1900	IL	CARROLL						1533		56		
"		1900	IL	"						150		36	SALEM TWP	✓
FISHER, EVAN SR	2/11	1830	PA	CHESTER				M19	148					
"	2/11	1850	"	"				M432	704	153			6. COUNTRY	
		copies so port Had to order from Chesson Press, PA							765,766					
WASTEN, D	2/8	1850	KY	CHRISTIAN				M432	196					
" ELIGAH	2/17	1840	KY	HOPKINS				M704	114					
"		1850	KY	MUHLENB				M432	214	191				
KNIGHT, JNC		1840	SC	C. CHESTER				M704	510	314				
"		1830	SC	CHESTERFIELD				M19	169,172					

SOUNDEX — SEVERAL NOS. MAY BE ON SAME REEL SUCH AS 621, 622, 623, ETC. FILE IS ARRANGED WITHIN NUMBER GROUPS BY FIRST NAME, ALPHABETICALLY. LAST NAME DOESN'T MATTER. FIND FIRST NAME, THEN CHECK FOR LAST NAME.

E.G. W623

18

WHERE TO KEEP YOUR RECORDS

Diary

A diary keeps your direction true when you first start. I kept it by each day I accomplished something and wrote down what I had done. I numbered the entries and cross-referenced the letters I wrote with my correspondence log (same number).

I also summarized my findings from a visit to the library or a trip to another area or just about anything I did relative to genealogy. I could recheck to see if everything was done on each item planned.

It's nice at the very beginning to help you get into focus; but as you start getting overwhelmed with material and get behind, it's easier to just use the correspondence log. After several years, I dropped the diary.

Censuses Ordered or Used

Keeping a list of censuses ordered or used from the National Archives in Washington, DC or from your library or other places (using the Census Indexes) will save you grief later from reordering the same census twice. (See Fig. 5.)

On your log of censuses ordered or used, note the name of person ordered for, year of film, state, county, Soundex number and code, film volume and reel or roll, sheet/line, Enumeration District (ED), town, date ordered, date received, results, etc. (See Chapter 8.) If you wish to reorder or to check something, it is simpler to find it on your log.

I ended up having a separate binder for census records with tab dividers for the states, with copies of the indexes for the names I was researching. Then I used tab dividers for individuals along with copies of the census information applicable to them.

Ledger

As you purchase your supplies, start keeping a record of cost in a ledger. When I reached the point of preparing to publish my genealogy, I had to go back and find all the costs of

19

putting it together, from equipment to supplies to duplicating photographs to research, plus cost of printing.

You will eventually develop your own system, but I hope this will give you a good start.

To Sum Up:

1. Label your manila folders with family name, last name capitalized, oldest ancestor first, with his children. Keep in box or file cabinet.

2. Label tab dividers same way. Put into binders that you prepared for each family, starting with oldest ancestor.

3. Put your pedigree charts in front of each binder and family group sheets behind each tab divider.

4. A sheet titled SEARCH for each family documenting progress may be inserted into the front of the manila folders and at the beginning of each section of the binders.

5. Documents can be kept in separate binders by family in archival sheet protectors.

6. Archival sheet protectors come in 8 1/2" x 11" and 8 1/2" x 14" sizes. There are also 8 1/2" x 14" binders. These items can be obtained in large office supply stores.

7. A steno pad or small notebook is useful to record date and place research was done.

8. You may want to keep data on 3x5 cards.

9. Prepare logs for Bibliography, Correspondence, Diary and Censuses Ordered or Used and keep in one or more binders.

10. Keep a record of your costs in a ledger as you may need this information at a later time.

P.S. A yellow hi-liter and white-out were very useful.

CHAPTER 3

PLACES YOU CAN DO RESEARCH

Before you start research, you have to find where to do it.

1. Search for the nearest Genealogy Room, which is usually in a library.

2. Search for other genealogical resources.

3. Find out what days and hours they are open and what you are allowed to take in.

4. Find out what resources are available there. If possible, get a listing of their holdings.

5. Visit research facilities in other cities where your ancestors lived.

6. Try to find living relatives in the cities you visit. You can search telephone books locally and inquire around.

7. Verify if previous research has been done on your family. Ask the Librarian to point out where this can be found.

8. You may want to join the local genealogical society. Later you might want to join the genealogical societies in the areas your ancestors lived.

Genealogy Rooms

Find out where the nearest Genealogy Room is. Usually it is in a library. Sometimes it is called by the state's name, such as Michigan Room or Maryland Room. A visit there would be helpful, to see how their books are kept, usually by state and county, and topic, such as ships' records, heraldry, military, etc. Records are also kept for foreign countries.

PLACES YOU CAN DO RESEARCH

The Librarian at the Reference Desk in your library can be very helpful or there may be a volunteer there to show you where to look.

You can see where new book arrivals are kept and the genealogy room card indexes. Most of the card catalog has been transferred to computers, of which there are usually several available. Information is kept by author, title or subject.

You can see where the census index books are and where you can use the microfilm and microfiche stored there. You can find out how you would order other films you might need.

Most genealogy rooms have shelves of family histories or genealogies prepared by members of local genealogical societies and those submitted by persons who have ancestors in the area.

Other Genealogical Resources

After you are familiar with your local library, look around the area for other available resources. Check if there are several libraries, like the city, county and university libraries, as well as where the State Archives and State Historical Society are located.

The Family History Library at the Church of Jesus Christ of Latter-day Saints (LDS), which is called the Mormon Church, is located in Salt Lake City, Utah. Branches of this library are in local LDS churches and are called family history centers, which are open to the public. They are listed in the phone book or at libraries. Volunteers there are very knowledgable.

The Family History Centers have records on microfiche (4" x 6" microfilm sheets), microfilm (in rolls) and on computer discs. They have readers for microfiche and reader/printers for microfilm. You can order microfilm from Salt Lake City when you find the number of the film you want.

They have a computer program, FamilySearch, which contains several files of family history information, such as the International Genealogical Index (IGI) what has 200 million names. The IGI is also on microfiche in file cabinets. Another computer file, the Family History Library Catalog, has about seven million names; there is also the Ancestral File, to which everyone may contribute their family history on diskettes. To learn how to do this, you can contact the local Family History Center.

Some of this information was submitted by researchers and may have errors. However, many original records, such as baptismal and marriage records, church registers, probate records, military records, land and tax records, have been photographed by their camera crews all over the world.

At my local Family History Center, I made a list of all the numbers of the microfilm I wanted to look at. When we traveled out west, we stopped at the Family History Library in Salt Lake City and I was able to look at all the film I had listed. There are very many files and microfilm readers. Some people come to spend weeks researching.

Days and Hours Open and What You Can Take In

Libraries and archives have certain days and times they are open, so you could call to check it out. The main library has information on libraries in all areas with their addresses and phone numbers.

Some genealogical rooms are separate from the main library, sometimes locked. Usually you cannot enter unless a volunteer is on duty. In some, you have to leave all your notes and materials in a locker or by the receptionist before you are allowed in, especially some State Archives. Some only allow pencils, not pens. They are so strict because some researchers have defaced books, cut pages from them or taken the whole books. However, it is hard to work without your notes.

There are photographic collections in some libraries and genealogical societies, but the ones I've seen are by date and not by person identified.

Each genealogy room is different. If you call ahead to check the days and hours, and what you are allowed to bring, you will be better prepared. Be sure to bring change for the copiers.

PLACES YOU CAN DO RESEARCH

Library Holdings

Some libraries and archives have a printed list of their holdings. They might include census indexes, censuses on microfilm, other microfilm, cemetery indexes, maps, county atlases, court records, indexes of births, deaths, marriages for various states, abstracts of wills, city directories, county histories, periodicals, genealogy manuals, etc.

This compiled information is usually in a file, a book or on the shelves by your state and other states, and other countries as well. Information is also available on CD's to be used at the library.

Remember that not all indexes include all names and sometimes they are in error, so several sources should be checked.

I found city directories for all years very helpful. Sometimes not all years have been collected, but you can still follow your ancestor's residence and occupation during the time he lived in the area.

A Phonedisc CD is in many libraries with names taken from phone directories all over the country. This data is divided by sections of the country and updated periodically.

Many libraries also have phonebooks from many other cities.

Research in Other Cities

If you are going to a different city to research, ask the Librarian the address and phone number for the library.

You could call to ask their hours and where they are located in the area. We like to call and ask for directions on how to get there and where the parking is. If you are planning to stay a few days, you may ask where the nearest lodging is. Everyone is very helpful. (See Chapter 11, Research Away from Home.)

Try to find living relatives in the areas you visit. Look in the local telephone books for your surname and ask around the town if your ancestor and his descendants are known.

PLACES YOU CAN DO RESEARCH

Previous Research

As you visit these areas, you might like to verify if anyone has done previous research on your family. You can ask the librarian to point out the indexes for published material.

Many libraries have the Periodical Source Index (<u>PERSI</u>), <u>Genealogical and Local History Books in Print</u> by Netti Schreiner-Yantis, and other indexes.

<u>PERSI</u> in an index of genealogical and historical periodical articles written in English and French since 1800. This index was created by the Allen County Public Library in Ft. Wayne, Indiana and is continually updated. At present it is in 27 volumes and many libraries own it. It is indexed by locality, family surname and/or research method. The <u>PERSI</u> is now available on CD-ROM on one disc.

When you find an article pertaining to your research, you may find the periodical it is in in your library or you may order it from the Allen County Public Library.

Family histories, genealogies and local histories may have information about your ancestors. Local histories have short biographies of well-known residents or early pioneers. However, information may have been submitted by family members and may not be accurate. Other records would have to be checked. Some local histories do not have indexes and you will have to read or scan all the way through.

At the Family History Library, you can check their records for previous research using the International Genealogical Index (IGI), Family Ancestry, etc.

Genealogical Societies

You may want to join the genealogical society nearest you. They have speakers at their meetings, workshops and genealogy classes. You may also want to join genealogical societies in the areas where your ancestors lived.

There are many genealogical societies. There is the National Genealogical Society in Arlington, Virginia, for the whole country. There are genealogical societies in each state and local societies for counties, cities, townships, etc., as well as ethnic societies, surname societies, and others.

Most have monthly newsletters, quarterly journals and bulletins, where members publish queries and new members list families they are researching. Book reviews are published of family histories and genealogical publications. Researchers submit extracts from old documents, cemetery readings of tombstones, and various topical subjects. Indexes and compilations of records are printed, as well as articles on genealogical matters.

Some societies, such as the National Genealogical Society and the Prince George's County Genealogical Society in Bowie, Maryland have lending libraries from which you can borrow books as a member, no matter where you live, for a small fee. You can check if the societies you are interested in have lending libraries.

Libraries or genealogy rooms should have a listing of these societies, as does the Handy Book.

Throughout the year, various genealogical societies have seminars for a day or more, with good programs, vendors of genealogical products, and contacts with other researchers. Notices are printed in the local paper, in their monthly newsletters or posted at the library. If you go to several, then notices will be sent directly to you.

To Sum Up:

1. Locate a genealogy room. See what their holdings are.

2. Check out if there are other genealogical resources, such as other libraries or archives. Find out when they are open and what you can take in.

3. Find if others have done research on your family.

4. Seek living relatives in cities you visit.

5. Join local genealogical societies; later you can join those where your ancestors were.

CHAPTER 4

STARTING RESEARCH

It's hard to say what sequence of research to follow. Do we look for vital records first or should we start with the census to see where our ancestors were? Should we look at wills and probates first because we have a death date or should we look at land records because we know where they lived at one time?

You don't always find records in the order you would like. You may find them in a random fashion and then pull what clues you can find and go back and fill in the gaps.

1. After you visit local libraries and state archives and search through indexes, local histories, censuses, and various other secondary (noted some time after the happening) materials, you can visit your county courthouse to see what primary (recorded at time of happening) records they have.

2. Secondary records, such as indexes, will lead you to primary records.

3. Note clearly who and what you will be looking for each time you go to a research facility.

4. You will be searching for documents that will have the information you want to input on your pedigree chart and family group sheet.

5. As you start your research, read the history of the area and of the country at the time you are researching to see what times were like when your ancestor lived there.

6. Get a good map book.

7. Investigate what records are kept at the National Archives.

8. Study the many helpful publications available.

STARTING RESEARCH

At the Library

At the library, you will be getting familiar with the records and indexes they have. Perhaps you already have some documents from your family and you can begin with the information there.

Look through books and indexes from the area and around the time your ancestor lived there. The state and county you are in will have the most thorough and greatest amount of material for your area. The census files are usually complete for your area, though not always so for others.

You should be able to collect some secondary records which will lead you to primary records.

Primary documents contain information that was given at the time it happened, such as birth or marriage certificates, census records, etc.

Secondary documents contain information that was given at another time or collected, such as in indexes, biographies, histories, etc. In other words, it is second-hand information, such as the birth information on a death certificate or a book with a collection of marriage records. These sources are used to find information in primary documents to verify them.

The County Courthouse

After you visit your library and state archives, you should visit your County Courthouse to see what records are kept there. What is kept varies with the states: there are birth, death and divorce records, marriage records, wills and probates, deeds, land records and various other records. These are mainly primary records, noted at the time events happened.

Some areas will allow you to look through the books and ledgers; in others, you have to request the clerk to find the documents.

Courthouses in some areas have genealogical society volunteers to help genealogists, but they are only there on certain days and hours, so you must call ahead.

Some local courthouses and county clerks have many records such as birth and death records from certain dates; marriage, divorce, probate and land records. However, in some states, probates and wills may be found with the county recorder or the probate clerk. Some land records may also be found at the Register of Deeds.

More recent birth, death, marriage and divorce records, though, are obtained in the Division of Vital Records or Bureau of Vital Statistics usually in the state capital or in a large city. Copies of these records or earlier records may be at the county clerk's office.

Because there is so much variation in where the records are kept in each state, to find the specific information, call your county courthouse or look in The Handy Book for Genealogists, published at Logan, Utah by Everton Publishers. It is updated periodically and can be found at any library or bookstore.

To Start:

You have prepared a place to put your findings, you have become familiar with your local library and the courthouse.

You will be searching for documents with information you want to input on your pedigree chart and family group sheet.

At the courthouse or other government office, you will be looking for:
Vital records, such as births, deaths, marriages and divorces
Wills and probates
Grantor (seller)--Grantee (buyer) Indexes
Deeds and land records
Tax records

Later, in various places, you will be looking for:
Federal Census records
Cemetery records
Church records
Obituaries and articles in newspapers

Later yet, you will be looking for:
Court records, abstracted and printed
Military records
Immigration records
Ships' Passenger Lists
And others

Vital Records Kept at County and State Level

Vital records are civil records of births, deaths, marriages and divorces; that is, they are kept in public repositories, such as county courthouses or state health departments, etc.

Vital records show relationships between persons.

Registering of births and deaths didn't become required till around the 1900's. Before that, records were in churches or in family bibles or other places. Marriage records were kept earlier, usually in the counties, as well as in churches. Some death records and other records are now closed to the public. Apparently, people were using them for criminal purposes. So check ahead.

Some states began keeping vital records earlier than others; therefore, each state's and county's holdings must be looked up individually. Sometimes the nearest court house was in the next county and that is where the records are.

The information on these records may not be accurate as, for example, women didn't give their correct ages on marriage records and the informant on death certificates may not have been sure of earlier information. The information taken at the time of the event, such as marriage date or death date or place of burial may be the most reliable.

You will find at times that the courthouse burned and the records are gone. Sometimes, they can be found in other ways; people kept some original records and some records had been copied in indexes; this would require a good deal of research.

Delayed birth certificates are kept in a separate book. These are certificates on which a person who had no birth

30

certificate fills out his birth date and place and must submit other documents verifying this is his age to establish a birthdate. Also, he must have a close relative or other person swear that this is true.

If you cannot find a record of death in indexes or at the courthouse, check the Family History Center computer or microfiche for death indexes. You can then order the microfilm if it is available. The death may have been in another area.

Another way to find death dates is to look at the Social Security Death Index. It is for people who had applied for Social Security from the time it started in 1937 and is kept by state and by birthdate. If they had not applied, they would not be on this index. It shows the date they died and where. This index is on CD's at various libraries and can be purchased from companies listed in genealogical magazines.

When you find the date of death, you may write to U.S. Social Security Office and get a copy of the original application, which shows when they applied, their parents, their birth date and place, what job they had at time of applying and residence. Sometimes you will see they had changed their names.

A Medical Family Tree

At this time, as you get death records and information, you may want to start a medical family tree, listing causes of death, date of onset of illness, cause of disease, how old the person was when he got sick.

Some of these conditions may be due to inherited genes. The more you are aware of genetic conditions in your family, the more you might be able to reduce some risks by a more healthful lifestyle.

There is a very good write-up on genetics in a special issue of the National Genealogical Society Quarterly in Volume 82, Number 2, June 1994, titled, <u>Your Family's Health History</u>.

Linking or Connecting Generations

It would be good at this time when you are at the beginning of your research to seek proof or establish probability that your father was his father's son by using various records. Then do the same for the preceding generations, linking each generation together. This will tie all generations back to the first ancestor found, authenticating your connection back to those ancestors.

I was researching about seven years when I found out that one has to establish linkage to one's ancestors. I had to look up which counties I had written to for birth or death records and which ones had said no, they didn't have any, among other things, before I could find the connections. This did take a lot of time, so it is better to be aware of this desired linkage early.

To Trace Your Line Back, Starting with a Death Certificate, for Example.

If you only know your grandfather's name and place of death, you could start with his death certificate. To find it, you can write to the courthouse in the county where he died. You can check indexes for that area at the Family History Library. You can write to the local library or local genealogical or historical societies checking for obituaries or indexes.

On a death certificate, there is usually a certificate number, the deceased's full name and residence; sex, race, if single, married, widowed or divorced; age and occupation; birthplace; his father's name, mother's maiden name and their birthplaces; date and place of death, probable cause of death, physician's or coroner's signature; name of undertaker, date and place of burial, informant, and county and state where filed.

Some information may not be too reliable; it may have been given by his wife or relative who wasn't sure of all facts.

In any case, you want to verify the death certificate bit by bit, by finding his will or probate; then, if possible, by visiting the cemetery where he was buried and seeing the gravestone and seeing the birth date, if it is on the stone. You may then try to locate his birth record and his marriage record. Then with those records, you may go back further.

After you contact the local county clerk and those in the counties where your ancestors were born, married and died, or you contact the State Vital Records Divisions, you should have some birth, marriage and death certificates.

Clerks in the courthouse are very busy and it is a favor to you for them to look up your information, even if you pay a small fee, so remember to send a stamped self-addressed envelope with your inquiry.

If possible, find out what the fee is ahead of time by calling the courthouse or checking in a U.S. government booklet, "Where to Write for Vital Records," and send it with your inquiry.

This booklet tells where, in each state, to send for vital records, such as for births, marriages, divorces and deaths, and the current fee. There is a phone number to call to inquire about any changes in address or fee if the booklet is a few years old. See it in your library or you can order it for a nominal fee from: Superintendent of Documents, Government Printing Office, Washington, DC 20402 (1993).

I would like to mention I would have saved time and steps when I queried various county offices for death certificates, birth certificates, etc. if I had done all my querying at once.

For example, I ordered a death certificate first, and received it. When I learned more about probate and wills, I ordered them a year later. The clerk wrote back, there is no probate, but there is a death certificate, which I already had. If I had asked for both at once, it would have saved writing twice.

Wills and Probates

After you find a date and place of death, you can look at the courthouse for a will, probate, inventory or appraisement.

A probate record relates to the disposition of an estate after the owner's death. Testate--left a will; Intestate--did not leave a will.

A will (See Fig. 6.) could be written years before a death. Usually, dates noted are the date the will was written and the

Fig. 6. Copy of a Will

Will of D. W. Wristen, with signature; page 1 of 6 only.
Taylor County Courthouse, Abilene, Texas. Book M, File 954,
pp. 18, 21. Abstract of will follows.

IN THE NAME OF GOD, AMEN:-

      I, D. W. Wristen, being of sound mind, and disposing memory, realising the uncertainty of life and the certainty of death, do make and publish this my LAST WILL AND TESTAMENT, hereby revoking any and all wills by me at any time heretofore made.

      ITEM ONE.

There are outstanding against me, at this time no money obligations worth mentioning nor will there likely be any at the date of my death, but what debts I owe, whether individual or community debts I wish my executor to pay, as shortly after my decease as is practicable.

      ITEM TWO.

I have heretofore conveyed to my wife Nettie Wristen, on the 12th. day of Jany. 1904, by my deed to her of that date, a life estate in my rock building, on Pine Street, Abilene, Texas, commonly known as "The Wristen Building", described as follows:-

      " Beginning at the N.E. corner of Lot No.7, Block No.2, Thence in a southerly direction, along the East boundary line of said Lot No.7, twenty-six feet. Thence in a westerly direction at right angles to the East line of said Block No.2, seventy-five feet, to the west Boundary line of Lot No.9, Block No.2, aforesaid. Thence in a northerly direction, along the west boundary line of Lot No.9, aforesaid, to its N.W. corner. Thence in an Easterly direction seventy-five feet to the place of beginning."

The life estate in said property above described was, as shown by my said deed to her, subject to be defeated by her subsequent remarriage, after my death, and in said deed I reserved the right to make disposition of the remaining interest in said property, which right it is my purpose now to do.

All my right, title, and interest in and to said above described property, (including the fee simple title, and the "remainder over " not covered by my said deed above mentioned) I will and bequeath unto my son D. W. Wristen, Jr., now an infant, PROVIDED HOWEVER, if my said son, D. W. Wristen, Jr., die before reaching his majority, then I will and bequeath said above described property, and all my right, title and interest therein to Frank R. Wristen, Ed M. Wristen, Mary L. Crowe, Thos. J. Wristen, Charles M. Wristen and Beulah Conner, share and share alike.

34

Fig. 7. Abstract of the Same Will

ABSTRACT OF LAST WILL AND TESTAMENT

Compiler __S. C. Fisher__   Surname __WRISTEN__

Address __5423 S. Dyewood Dr.__   Date Abstracted __1987__

__Flint, MI 48532-3328__

County __Taylor__   State __Texas__

Will Book __M   File 954__   Page __18, 21__

Court/Repository __Taylor County Courthouse, Abilene, Texas__

Testator __D. W. Wristen__

Place of Residence __Abilene, Taylor County, Texas__

Personal Information __Date of death - September 16, 1918__

Executor(s) __Ed M. Wristen__

Date Signed __March 2, 1910__   Date Proved __October 25, 1918__

Signature or Mark __D. W. Wristen, his signature__

Witnesses __Will J. Schultz   Sue R. Smith__

Bequests, Devises, etc. __To wife, Nettie Wristen, life estate in Rock Building, "The Wristen__
Building," on Pine Street, Abilene, Texas, until remarriage.

to son D. W. Wristen, Jr., an infant, remaining interest in above property, subject

to provision if he die before reaching majority, property to Frank R. Wristen,

Ed M. Wristen, Mary L. Crowe, Thos. J. Wristen, Charles M. Wristen and Beulah

Conner, share and share alike.

To Nettie Wristen, all household furnishings and other items, she already having

received 330 acres in Callahan County, Texas by deed dated February 6, 1906.

Remaining estate divided into 50 shares to children: son Frank R. Wristen,

8 shares, Ed M. Wristen 3 shares, daughter Diluly I. White, 6 shares, daughter

Mary L. Crowe, 7 shares, son Thos. J. Wristen, 6 shares, son Charlie M. Wristen,

8 shares, daughter Beulah B. Conner, 8 shares. Those of my children not

named, I have heretofore given them all which it seems to me they are justly

and fairly entitled to receive, and I hope they will so regard it.

date the will was proved or executed. This would show the approximate date of death. The named executor or executors will settle the estate, by paying debts and taxes, dividing the estate among heirs, etc.

If someone died without a will, an interested person, such as a spouse, can apply for Letters of Administration to settle the estate.

Children who are beneficiaries are named in sequence. Also named are those who had been taken care of previously. Daughters are listed by their married names; previous places of residence may be noted; clues to profession may be in the inventory listed, such as blacksmith's tools, or farming tools and animals. Witnesses may be relatives. If land is bequeathed, the location is noted.

A Will Abstract

To abstract a will, you may use available forms or a plain piece of paper. Note the name of the county and state, which willbook you found the will in and the page number. Write the name of the person who died, date, where buried. Write the date the will was written and when it was proved. Name each person in the will, relation to the testator and their bequest in detail. Write the names of the executor(s) and the witnesses. List what was in the inventory, any action taken and the final settlement. (See Fig.7.)

Inventories and appraisements are very interesting because they shed light on what life was like. Old inventories list the clothing left, the type it was, the household items, the tools of the trade and perhaps some dear items, like a gold buckle or good book. They also show debts owed and to whom.

To find probate records, look in counties where probated or in the nearest courthouse which might be in a nearby county.

At the courthouse, find out where they have wills, probates and inventories. The wills are usually recorded in ledgers that you can look at. The ledgers are stored by year.

Probate files and probate papers are stored variously. At one courthouse, the probate papers were kept in the basement in little boxes, and so named, box so and so.

We found some tied with string in bundles, called file #___.

When you are researching, you will notice documents with your ancestor's name spelled several different ways in the same document and spelled other ways in other documents. It is quite a challenge to find out if this is the same person.

Census takers, clerks, lawyers, etc. may have spelled some names based on how they sounded. Many people were illiterate and didn't know how to spell their name. Names could have been copied wrongly into indexes. Some people changed their names as time went by. You will probably find many spellings and usually it is best to copy them as spelled and later to seek more verification.

Probate records are listed in published indexes and abstracts, and on microfilm. These can be found at state archives and libraries and at the LDS Family History Centers.

Land Records

Land records are more fully discussed in Chapter 10.

Some land records are at the county court house, at the Registrar of Deeds. This department is also called Office of the County Recorder, Clerk of the Circuit Court or other name.

Land records are kept by the grantor (seller)-grantee (buyer) indexes. After you find a name in the index, you can search the ledgers where deeds and other documents are recorded. They are usually handwritten. If you find a pertinent document, someone will take the ledger and make a copy for you. The original is with the grantor or grantee.

Older Documents

You should know that very old documents, like wills, deeds, indentures, etc., were all written by hand and copied by hand. Some are in beautiful clear writing; others are scrawled with words misspelled and names hard to read. Some handwriting has faded. Some copies are so poor and dark that very little can be read. Errors were made in names, dates, etc. In recent years, documents are printed or typed, with blanks for names and other information.

Fig. 8. Transcription and An Old Handwritten Document

INDENTURE
3 January 1825, Book Y, pp. 197, 8
Anson County Courthouse, NC
(Copied and transcribed March 1992)

John Hendricks, James Womble and Temperance
His Wife and Nancy Hendricks to Jesse Duran

This Indenture made this 3d day of January 1825 between John Hendricks, James Womble and Temperance, his wife and Nancy Hendricks of one part and Jesse Duran of the other part, witnesseth that the said John Hendricks, James Womble and Temperance his wife and Nancy Hendricks for and in consideration of the sum of six hundred dollars to them in hand paid by the said Jesse Duran Hath Bargained sold aliened enfrossed conveyed and confirmed and doth by these presents Bargain, sell, alien, enfroff, convey and confirm unto the said Jesse Duran, his heirs and assigns, all their undivided parts of a certain tract of land situate in the County of Anson containing three hundred and fifty acres adjoining the lands of William Rorie, James Rorie being the same land which Gustavus Hendricks died seized of and willed to his children said tract into seven equal parts to be divided To Have and To Hold all the said John Hendricks, James Womble and Temperance his wife and Nancy Hendricks' rights to the aforesaid tract of land to him the said Jesse Duran his heirs and assigns forever and the said John Hendricks, James Womble Temperance his wife and Nancy Hendricks doth hereby each warrant and defend their respective undivided shares of the aforesaid tract of land unto him the said Jesse Duran his heirs and assigns against the lawful claim of all persons whatsoever in witness whereof the said John Hendricks, James Womble and Temperance his wife and Nancy Hendricks have hereunto set their hands and seals the date first above written, signed sealed and delivered in the presence of A. Sinclair, A. Wimberly, Anson, July 1832. Then this deed was duly proven in open court by A. Sinclair and ordered to be registered.

s/ John Hendricks, Nancy G. Hendricks,
James Womble, Temperance (X-her mark) Womble
s/ W. Disweeker, Clk.

Below is a copy of the original indenture from which the above was transcribed:

38

You may find your ancestors' signatures on these documents, usually noted as that they set their hands and seals on the date first above written. (See Fig. 8.) Other times, if you check the signatures on these documents, you will note that some are in the same handwriting as the body of the document. That usually signified that the writer (court clerk, lawyer, etc.) also signed the document. Your ancestor then placed his "X" and a notation said "his seal." On Figure 8, one person did put her mark.

Later Records

Records you will be looking at later, such as Federal Census records, cemetery records, church records, obituaries and articles in newspapers are discussed in later chapters.

Further Records You Will Search Later (Discussed Very Briefly as They Entail More Advanced Research)

Other Court Records

There are so many various court proceedings that this should be a separate study. Court records cover many events in the life of an area. There are civil and criminal courts. There are some indexes to court cases and printed records. There are chancery courts, orphans' courts and prerogative courts, etc.

Military Records

Military records, which include pension, service and bounty-land records, can be obtained from the National Archives. Forms are available in the library or directly from the National Archives: NATF Form 80, Order for Copies of Veterans Records (1994).

Some information on your ancestor is required to fill out the applications, such as, name of the soldier, the war and time he served, where he enlisted, etc. A fee is charged.

These procedures are fully discussed in most how-to books.

Immigration Records and Ships' Passenger Lists

Also discussed more fully in how-to books are various immigration records.

Fig. 9.

MIGRATION TRAIL OF THE RISTON-WRISTEN FAMILY

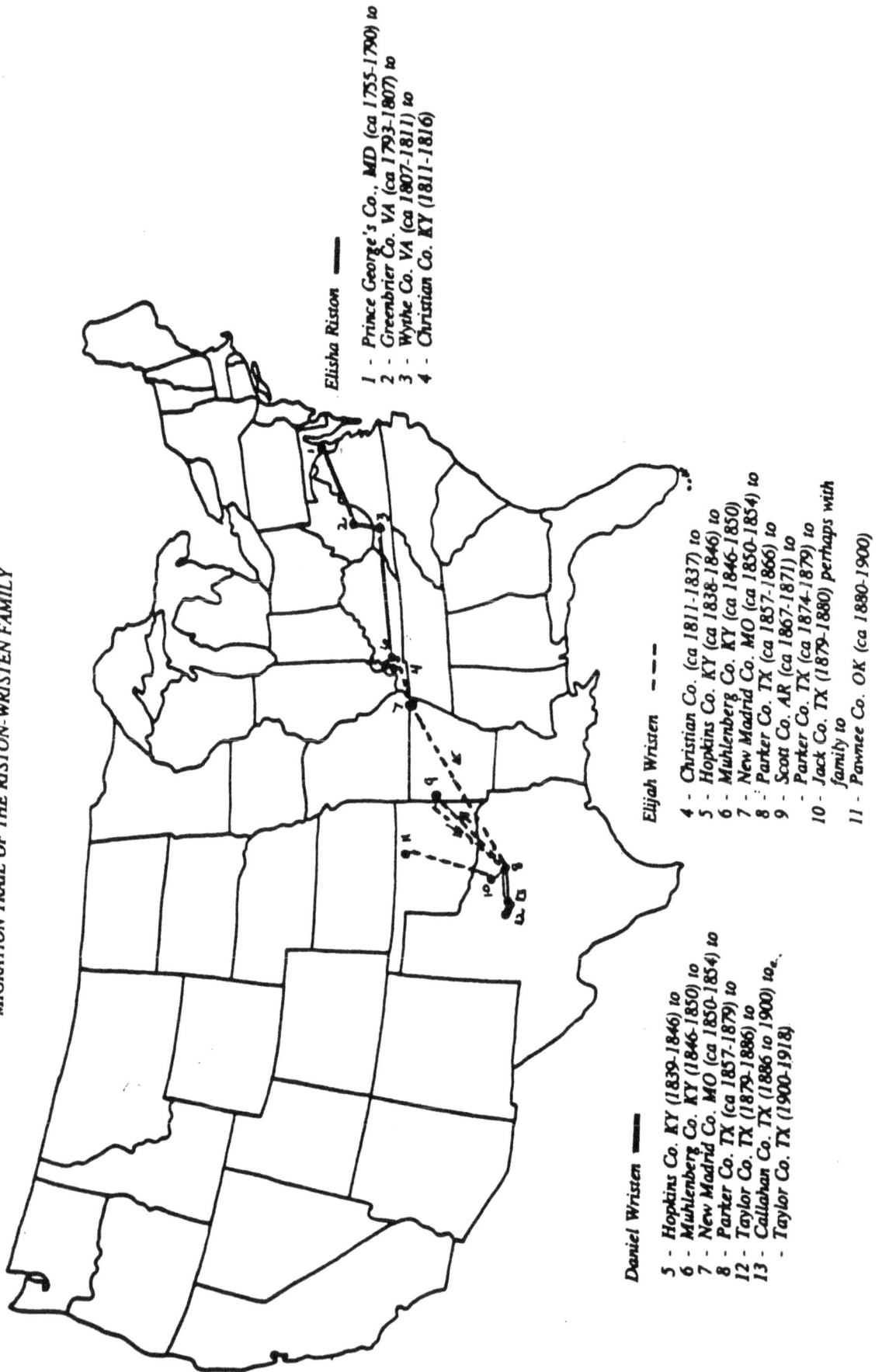

Elisha Riston ▬▬▬

1 - Prince George's Co., MD (ca 1755-1790) to
2 - Greenbrier Co. VA (ca 1793-1807) to
3 - Wythe Co. VA (ca 1807-1811) to
4 - Christian Co. KY (1811-1816)

Elijah Wristen ▬ ▬ ▬

4 - Christian Co. (ca 1811-1837) to
5 - Hopkins Co. KY (ca 1838-1846) to
6 - Muhlenberg Co. KY (ca 1846-1850) to
7 - New Madrid Co. MO (ca 1850-1854) to
8 - Parker Co. TX (ca 1857-1866) to
9 - Scott Co. AR (ca 1867-1871) to
10 - Parker Co. TX (ca 1874-1879) to
10 - Jack Co. TX (1879-1880) perhaps with
       family to
11 - Pawnee Co. OK (ca 1880-1900)

Daniel Wristen ▬▬▬

5 - Hopkins Co. KY (1839-1846) to
6 - Muhlenberg Co. KY (1846-1850) to
7 - New Madrid Co. MO (ca 1850-1854) to
8 - Parker Co. TX (ca 1857-1879) to
12 - Taylor Co. TX (1879-1886) to
13 - Callahan Co. TX (1886 to 1900) to
13 - Taylor Co. TX (1900-1918)

40

Listings of ships' passenger lists are in libraries and other repositories. If you know or find the ship and the month and year your ancestor arrived here, you can submit a form to the National Archives to get a copy of the ship's passenger list with your ancestor's name on it plus other information. The most recent forms are at your library or the National Archives.

At the Family History Library of The Church of Jesus Christ of Latter-day Saints (LDS), microfilm can be ordered of the Soundex copies of ships' passenger lists and has to be gone through card by card looking for your ancestor's name. These Soundex cards are coded and have to be interpreted by someone familiar with them at the Center.

Local History

Find as much as you can in your library about the area where your ancestors lived. Search out any local histories written about the early citizens. A Bibliography of American County Histories by W. F. Filby, lists towns where local histories were written. In The Handy Book, asterisks denote in each county if there were county histories written.

Map Books and Collections

Libraries have early map books and collections of maps which show rivers, post offices, churches, and early settlements, some with names of early settlers. Also check for old atlases and maps at the courthouse and other government buildings.

The Guide to Genealogical Research in the National Archives lists a large amount of various types of maps in their Cartographic Section which you can order.

The Migration Pattern

As you find out more about your family from vital records, censuses, land and tax records, and study maps of where they lived and traveled, you can plot their migration pattern--the routes taken, the early roads, such as the Wilderness Trail, and areas they passed through. (See Fig. 9.)

STARTING RESEARCH

The National Archives

The <u>Guide to Genealogical Research in the National Archives</u>, published by the National Trust Fund Board for the National Archives in Washington, D.C. shows how to order various records and what information is included in each.

There is a wealth of information about maps, censuses, general land office records, military records, immigration, ships passenger Arrival Lists, and many more categories. This book goes into great depth to explain holdings and methods and how to access them. It is available at libraries, archives, genealogical seminars, etc. or it can be purchased from the National Archives.

For example, in the section on various military records, it is noted that Civil War records are divided into Confederate and Union military personnel. They are listed by state in which enlisted.

Helpful Publications

<u>The Handy Book for Genealogists</u>, published by the Everton Publishers, Inc., PO Box 368, Logan, Utah 84321, lists alphabetically by state and county where the government offices are that keep records, with the address of the county seat and zip code. Foreign countries are listed after states.

This book notes county clerks, court recorders, etc. and what vital records are stored in each area for which years. They also list if there are land, court and miscellaneous records as well as many genealogical sources. There is a map for each state with the counties shown and much other information.

The latest issue is available in the library. This was the first book I purchased.

As aforementioned, I also found invaluable a booklet from the U.S. Government, "Where to Write for Vital Records." It tells where, in each state, to send for vital records, such as for births, marriages, divorces and deaths, and the current fee.

There is a phone number to call to inquire about any changes in address or fee if the booklet is a few years old. See it in

your library or you can order it for a nominal fee from:
Superintendent of Documents, Government Printing Office,
Washington, DC 20402 (1993).

An excellent reference book is The Source: A Guidebook of
American Genealogy by Arlene Eakle and Johni Cerny, published
by Ancestry Publishing Company, Salt Lake City. It covers
vital records, the topics above and many other aspects of
genealogical research. It is in libraries and can also be
purchased. It has been updated in 1997.

Another good reference book is The Library A Guide to the LDS
Family History Library, edited by Johni Cerny & Wendy Elliott,
Ancestry Publishers, Salt Lake City, UT 84110.

An interesting informative publication is the Genealogy
Bulletin put out by the AGLL Genealogical Services, P.O. Box
329, 593 West 100 North Bountiful, Utah 84011-000329. This
company also issues Heritage Quest of the same address. Both
publications are good. The Bulletin goes into different phases
of research in depth. Perhaps your library carries these
publications or they can be subscribed to.

I never knew these publications existed until I took a class
offered by my genealogical society on how to construct a
family tree. It is hard for an individual to find out anything
and takes a long time to gather all this information together.

As you gather data and information from these sources, be sure
to analyze it to be sure it is relative to your previous
research.

To Sum Up:

1. After you visit your local libraries, you can visit the courthouse, where, using data from indexes, censuses, etc., you can look for vital records, deeds, wills, probates, etc.

2. See The Handy Book by Everton and the U.S. Government publication, "Where to Write for Vital Records" at your library, or you may want to purchase these.

3. Remember that not all areas have all the records. Each repository has different records which have to be located.

4. As you research, remember secondary records like indexes will lead you to primary records like marriage records.

5. Analyze your gathered material to be sure it is relevant to your research. Evaluate the evidence to see if it is probable. Check conflicting information.

6. Now is the time to establish linkage to previous generations.

7. Read local histories and local history of the area where your ancestors were located.

8. Investigate maps.

9. Investigate what is available at the National Archives.

10. Check out helpful publications.

CHAPTER 5

CORRESPONDENCE AND QUERIES

As you begin to get an idea where the records are and have started to gather a few, you will be writing to various places.

1. Set up a correspondence log. Keep it in a binder.

2. Number each letter. Log it in with date and number. If you keep a copy, number it. If not, write a summary on the log.

3. Keep the copy in a pending file where you can check progress. After a period of time, if you don't receive a reply, a follow-up is in order.

4. If you do receive a reply, note date received and result on the log. File the reply in the correspondence log binder with the copy.

5. Try to be prompt in answering correspondence. One week seems reasonable.

6. Check Query sections in genealogical magazines and society publications. You can search for someone working on the same line as you are and submit a query of your own.

7. Keep a record of what cost is involved, if any.

Who are you going to write to?

The first letters may be to your distant relatives. Then you may be writing to state and county offices. Later, you might be answering and submitting queries.

Fig. 10. A Genealogical Letter

5423 S. Dyewood Dr.
Flint, MI 48532
February 13, 1990
(313) 731-0000

Marylyn Smith
P.O. Box 234
Anywhere, MD 20201

Dear Marylyn,

I saw your query in the Genealogical Helper of Sept-Oct 1989.

I am also researching the Knight family and listed below is
what we have found so far in my husband's line.

My husband's great grandfather, James Malcolm Calloway Knight
(1821-1898) was first seen in the 1850 Census for Marlboro
County, SC, with wife Susannah Womble (1833-1897) and one
child, Mary, 1 year old. From the census, he was shown as
born in South Carolina and she in North Carolina.

They traveled south to Alabama (1860), Arkansas (1870), and
finally Texas (1880) where they are both buried in Buffalo
Gap, Taylor Co. and it was from their tombstone that I got
their birth and death dates.

I have not been able to find their parents, place of birth and
marriage date, but I'll be happy to share what I have found.

Hoping to hear from you,

Sincerely,

Sophie Fisher

Enc.

CORRESPONDENCE AND QUERIES

Writing the Letter

1. Be specific, brief and friendly. State what you are looking for in the least amount of words, with short paragraphs. (See Fig. 10.)

2. Make your letter clear and easy to understand. Those not working on genealogy, such as some of your relatives, are unfamiliar with some terms and may wonder why you are asking for this information. You may want to explain your purpose.

3. Try to ask for facts for one family at a time.

4. Mention a few facts you have, but not too many, as that discourages many from answering.

5. Ask what line they are following and that you would be happy to share what you have found.

6. I found many don't answer, even if you send a stamped self-addressed envelope. I realize they are under no obligation to respond just because I wrote to them.

7. If it appears that the correspondent might have some of the information you would want, send a follow-up letter within a reasonable time.

8. Write a thank-you note to anyone who gives you needed information.

9. Offer to pay for any copies you ask for.

10. When writing to libraries, if you ask them to search for you, it is appreciated if you send a donation along.

11. When corresponding with professional researchers, it is always good to specify your limit on hours to be researched at first; otherwise, the fee might be large.

At first, I kept a correspondence log and a diary of what I did each day, including the letters I had sent. I kept copies of all the letters I wrote, gave them numbers and entered them in the correspondence log, as well in the diary.

Fig. 11. A Copy of A Shell Document for Fisher-LET-2

5423 S. Dyewood Dr.
Flint, MI 48532
May 7, 1990
(313) 731-0000

NAME

DEAR

This is in reponse to your query in the Genealogical Helper of
Sept-Oct 1989.

I am also researching the Fisher family and listed below is what we
have found so far in my husband's line.

Francis STANFIELD (1648?-1692) m. Grace _____(England)
William HUNTLEY   (1668?-1708) m. Mary STANFIELD -1692-PA
Thomas FISHER   (1684-1747) m. Elizabeth HUNTLEY-1713/4-PA
Elizabeth FISHER (1718-c1800) m. Joseph WILKINSON -1740-PA

I would appreciate any information you might have as to where
Thomas Fisher was born or came from. Any information, though, on
the above families would be appreciated and I'll be happy to send
any information I have.

Hoping to hear from you,

Sincerely,

Sophie Fisher

Enc.
LET-2

48

This took too much time and paper. I gave up my diary. Now I only make copies of complex letters or those with much information. The others, I just list by name, number and context in my log. With my log and a pending file, I can check the status of research and correspondence.

After writing various letters, you may find you can't find the copies when you want to refer to them. Even if they are listed in the correspondence log, you are not sure where you filed them.

I ended up putting most of the copies of my letters and the replies in the file of the person they were about. This way I could usually find them. In the log book, I put in what file the letters were kept.

You could list all your correspondents' names, addresses and phone numbers and keep them in front of your folders.

If You Are Using a Computer

If you are using a computer now or are planning to get one, I'd like to share my system of correspondence with you.

When I got a computer, I started a system where I made a shell document for each surname I was researching and summarized the most pertinent facts I had and was seeking.

I named or numbered each document Let-1, Let-2, etc. then Let-1A, Let-1B, etc. for each surname, but any name or number could be used. I kept a list of surname and document names, like LET-2 was Fisher and LET-2R was Riston. (See Fig. 11.)

I kept these document names and surnames on a list. This way I could just pull up the letter for the surname wanted and change it to suit the correspondent, using the same basic information.

On the first page of each family's correspondence on my computer, I listed the names, addresses and phone numbers of all my correspondents and what line of the family they were following. Many are now including their E-Mail addresses.

Fig. 12. A Submitted Query

QUERY TO
THE SOUTH CAROLINA MAGAZINE OF ANCESTRAL RESEARCH

KNIGHT-WOMBLE-GWYNN-HENDRICHS. Mrs. Robert W. Fisher, 5423 S. Dyewood Dr., Flint, MI 48532. Seeks parents, siblings birthplace and marriage date of James Malcolm Callaway Knight (b.1821, SC or NC, d. 1898, Buffalo Gap, TX.) Married Susannah Womble, (b.1833 NC, d. 1897 TX) dau of Henry Womble (1791-1855) and Jane Gwynn. Henry was son of James Womble and Temperance Hendrichs. James Knight, Susannah and Mary, 1 yr old, are shown on the US Census 1850, Marlboro Co., SC. His occupation shown as Overseer. Does anyone know of any plantations he could have been on in this area?

Mrs. R. W. Fisher

The Query in Print in Volume XX, Number 1. Winter 1992.

KNIGHT-WOMBLE-GWYNN-HENDRICHS. Mrs. Robert W. Fisher (5423 S. Dyewood Dr., Flint, MI 48523) seeks parents, siblings, birthplace and marriage date of James Malcolm Callaway Knight (born 1821, SC or NC, d. 1890B, Buffalo Gap, TX). He married Susannah Womble (b. 1833, NC, d. 1897, TX) dau of Henry Womble (1791-1855) and Jane Gwynn. Henry was a son of James Womble and Temperance Hendrichs. James Knight, Susannah, and Mary, 1 year old, are shown on the 1850 census of Marlboro Dist., SC. His occupation indicated as overseer. Does anyone know of any plantations on which he could have been in this area?

CORRESPONDENCE AND QUERIES

Queries

When you read the <u>Genealogical Helper</u> by Everton, you will notice various sections involving queries: Computerized "Roots" Cellar, Bureau of Missing Ancestors, Missing Folk Finder, etc. This was the first publication I subscribed to and received much information in answer to my submissions.

If you subscribe to other genealogical publications, such as <u>Heritage</u> or <u>Ancestry</u>, you will notice they have a query section also.

Most genealogical newsletters and some quarterlies have query sections. You may want to visit the library's genealogical room, and check out queries in copies of quarterlies and newsletters for many state and county genealogical societies.

Submitting Queries

You may want to put in queries of your own. Some have to be paid for; others are free to subscribers. Abbreviations can be used on some queries; others are required to be spelled out, with the editor doing the abbreviations.

The query should be brief and to the point. The query should state the surname, period or date, and locality you are seeking. It can be about one surname or several. Be specific about what information you are seeking and list some information you already have. (See Fig. 12.)

It is more effective if you query about one family.

I kept queries in a separate binder, numbering them and noting on a log sheet when submitted, to which publication and when published. I copied their printed page, numbered it and kept it in the binder, with the query.

I have to admit, when I first started, I got most of my information from researchers when I answered their queries. And I still get a good response when I submit queries.

Also, if you are using a computer, a format can be set up for queries for each surname you are researching. When I wanted to submit a query, the letter could be changed or arranged, but the basic information was there.

To Sum Up:

1. Keep a correspondence log. Number your letters.

2. Write letters to relatives and other researchers; write to county and state offices, libraries, etc., and finally to professional researchers, if necessary.

3. Be specific and brief. Ask, "What line are you following?"

4. Log in each letter with date and number. Number the copy or write a summary in the log.

5. Keep the copy in a pending file. Note on the log if you receive a reply. If not, write a follow-up letter.

6. Respond quickly to correspondence.

7. Write and answer queries.

8. If you are using a computer, you can make shell documents for your genealogical letters and queries and keep lists of document names and numbers.

9. Keep a record of the cost of paper, postage, researchers' fees, cost of subscriptions to genealogical publications. If using a computer and printer, note cost of each, toners, etc.

CHAPTER 6

ORGANIZING YOUR MATERIAL

1. The main objective in organizing your material is so it is at the ready when you need it.

2. One of the goals is that it will be easy to handle and follow when you begin to put together the story of your family.

3. Another goal is that you can see where you left off in case you have to put your research aside for a while.

4. The long-range goal is that anyone can step up and understand your method of organization and be able to use it if you decide to pass it on to another researcher.

It is very important to keep meticulous records and not in too many places. Have one main place that you always update, and use that as your basis to update the rest of your records. As you get more information together, you may wish to input it on a genealogical computer program.

An overall summary is very helpful.

The best way to stay organized and keep track of what you have done, what you have, and what you need, is to start a running summary of all, like a story (besides the individual summaries) and tell where you went and what you saw, who you called, what you read and what you found and where it is.

Otherwise, you may have to go back and put it together by rereading all the material, as I had to do, to get a perspective over it all.

Each time you work on your genealogy, STOP and enter all the data you obtained into your binders and your logsheets and your summaries. Keep current.

ORGANIZING YOUR MATERIAL

Several years after I had put down a lot of information, I read that it was not a true pedigree unless everything on it was factually documented, so I had to look up all my facts again to be sure they had a basis and write them all down. If only I had known, I would have started with the first fact.

You have prepared your storage places and checked out the repositories of material you will want to see. You have collected some documents. You want to document data as you go and know it helps to be organized.

To Sum Up:

1. Organize your material so it will be ready when you need it, you can see where you are in your research, and anyone else will be able to pick up where you left off.

2. Prepare to keep a main record that is always updated.

3. Keep a running summary, like a story, of all you are doing, besides the individual summaries.

4. Don't forget to document the source of each fact.

5. Keep a record of the cost of postage, writing materials, inter-library loans.

CHAPTER 7

DOCUMENTING YOUR INFORMATION

1. Documenting your information means that for every fact you put down, you have to write down exactly from what source you got it, and where and when you got it. Every item you enter should have a basis somewhere.

2. Someone else should be able to look at your documentation and go to the same place to see the same information.

3. The documentation should be plainly written and easy to understand. This is called citing.

4. There are many formats for citations, depending on what the source is.

5. As you go into various sources, check the information you obtain to be sure it is the right information for your family. Analyze any evidence from sources to see if it is probable and merits more research.

6. Don't put down a date or fact that you are not sure of or if there is conjecture or conflicting information without putting down a question mark and/or explanation.

Though I searched many books, it was very difficult to understand how to go about getting the documents necessary to verify information and how to write down the sources.

Sources

There are many sources for the genealogist: vital records, wills, probates, cemetery records, land records, published sources, such as indexes, periodicals, newspapers,etc., bibles, family histories, local histories, unpublished manuscripts, pedigree charts of others, military documents, census records, microfilm records, and many others.

DOCUMENTING YOUR INFORMATION

You need verify and document the information from these sources and enter it on your pedigree charts, family group sheets and in your files. Also, you can enter it on your summary search sheets for each person or family.

How to Cite Your Documents

Write a citation on each of the documents, or copies, you accumulate, showing what the source is, where it is located, volume, page number, certificate number and date, who produced it, and when and where you saw it, such as:

> Will of D. W. Wristen, 25 Oct. 1918. Taylor County Courthouse, Abilene, Texas, Book M, File 954, pp. 18, 21, copied by S. Fisher 1987.

Another example of a citation:

> Marriage License issued in Prince George's County, Maryland, for Elisha Riston and Ann Mayoh, 7 February 1790, found in the King George's Parish Register 1689-1801, page 265, at the Maryland State Archives, Annapolis, Maryland, by S. Fisher, in May, 1990.

You or anyone else has to be able to find the exact document again from which you got the information.

Formats for Citations

Standard forms of citation should be used for documenting genealogical sources, according to Richard S. Lackey in his book, Cite Your Sources: A Manual for Documenting Family Histories and Genealogical Records printed in 1980 by the University Press of Mississippi in Jackson, Mississippi.

There are different forms for the various kinds of sources. Published sources are cited differently from original sources; sources cited in bibliographies and footnotes have different formats as to placement and punctuation.

Citations for periodicals, newspapers, microfilm records and other records each use different punctuation and formats.

DOCUMENTING YOUR INFORMATION

These citations basically show what the source is, where it is located, who produced it and when, as noted previously. But, without a reference, it is difficult to tell which format to use.

I suggest you would do better to refer to Mr. Lackey's book, which has been updated, as well as the many written since 1980 and available in most libraries.

I bought his book for reference because it's too hard to remember all these variations.

If, later, you might try to put together a family history, it would be more efficient if the citations were in the right genealogical form to start.

This is one of the things I didn't do and had to go back and add a citation to each of my documents. I had to sort thru my data, check all the dates and discrepancies and try to get down to the essence.

Cite as you go.

Questionable Sources

You should cite all the data or tell why not. Put a question mark where you are in doubt, aren't sure of the information or are making an estimate.

Some researchers put down information someone sent them and then pass it on to someone else with no question marks, explanations or documentation. This is the way wrong information is spread to a great number of people who then try to puzzle it out.

Analyzing the Evidence from Your Sources

After 10 years, I learned that all the evidence from sources for each event should be analyzed on how probable it is, or if it's more probable than not, by a variety of proofs: dates on death certificates, names and dates in index books, etc.

Instances have been found where a child is listed as born before her mother, which obviously is improbable; so check your dates very carefully.

DOCUMENTING YOUR INFORMATION

To me, the most important thing about documenting your information is that dates and facts should be verified and analyzed. If there is a doubt, question marks should be used and an explanation offered.

To Sum Up:

1   Write a citation on all your documents.

2. Be sure another person can use your documentation to find the same information.

3. Check all dates and facts to verify they are feasible.

4. If you are not sure or couldn't get enough documentation for your data, use a question mark and explanation.

5. If someone sent you data without documentation, try to verify it or use it with a question mark.

6. Get a good reference book on how to cite your sources.

CHAPTER 8

FEDERAL CENSUS RECORDS

1. The Federal Population Census has been taken every 10 years since 1790.

2. Catalogs of the Federal Population Census Schedules for 1790-1890 and for 1900, 1910 and 1920 are available from the National Archives in Washington, D.C. Most of the 1890 Federal Population Census was destroyed by fire, but the partial censuses left are listed in the 1790-1890 catalog.

3. The 1920 Federal Population Census is the latest opened and would be a good place to start research. Previous censuses can then be searched working back in time.

4. Population Census Index Books are available for every state, though not for every year, with surnames in alphabetical order, showing county, page and township where these individuals are located in the census.

5. The 1880 Population Census was the first indexed according to the Soundex system, where last names are grouped together by the way they sound, not by how they are spelled. The Soundex listings are in the same catalogs as the Federal Population Census.

6. Census forms or worksheets are available for each year of the census on which to copy extracted information from the microfilm. The microfilm itself can be copied if certain pages have to be referred to again.

7. Other Federal Census Schedules are for mortality, agriculture, industry, manufacturing; slave schedules; the 1840 census of Revolutionary War pensioners and others.

8. A complete listing should be kept of each roll ordered, its cost, when and where it was found and result.

FEDERAL CENSUS RECORDS

The Federal Population Census is an enumeration of population as provided for in the Constitution. It has been taken every 10 years since 1790.

Federal Population Census Catalogs

There are catalogs of Federal Population Census Schedules available on National Archives microfilm for 1790-1890 and for 1900, 1910 and 1920. Though most of the 1890 census was destroyed by fire, the partial censuses left are noted in the 1790-1890 population census catalog.

Each catalog of the Federal Population Census has much more information than just listings of states and rolls of film.

In the catalog for 1790-1890, the introduction gives a description of the schedules; finding aids are listed, as is availability of other catalogs relating to research interests, such as American Indians, Immigrant and Passenger Arrivals, etc. There is the 1880 Soundex Index and a guide for using it; special schedules (1890) enumerating Union veterans, widows of Union veterans of the Civil War, and order forms for microfilm.

The catalog for 1900 has the 1900 Soundex Index, a guide for using it, abbreviations used in the Soundex and order forms.

The catalog for 1910 has the 1910 Soundex Index for 21 states and a guide for using it. Microfilm Publication T1224 is listed as giving Census Enumeration District Descriptions.

Appendix I of the 1910 catalog gives a Guide to the Soundex/Miracode System, (for some states and are so labeled); Appendix II gives Relationship Terms and Abbreviations and Appendix III gives Enumeration Districts within Cities Having Populations of 50,000 or More.

The catalog for 1920 has more detailed descriptions of the 1920 schedules, the Soundex and Enumeration Districts, as well as Research Hints, the 1920 Soundex Index and order forms. These catalogs are available at libraries, archives, etc.

Available microfilm copies of the censuses listed can be ordered through the Census Microfilm Rental Program.

60

FEDERAL CENSUS RECORDS

For a nominal fee, you can purchase these catalogs from the Publications Services Branch (NEPS), National Archives, Washington,DC 20408.

In these catalogs, each year of the census is given an identifying number, such as, the First Census of the United States, 1790, is M637 and the 10th Census, 1880, is T9.

States, territories and some large cities are listed alphabetically by year; under them, counties are listed by identifying number individually or in groups, such as, for Kentucky in 1880, Adair, Allen, Anderson and Ballard Counties are Number 401. So when you order film for that location, you would write, T9, Roll 401.

The numbers for the rolls start with 1 for each year and continue for the number of rolls available for that year; for example, 1,454 rolls for 1880 are noted in the catalog.

At the beginning of each roll of microfilm is a list of the counties therein, so you can tell where on the roll the county is you are searching for--at the beginning, end or in-between.

The county will be listed at the top of the microfilmed census sheet and sometimes the town or post office will be listed. You can then search page by page and house by house. Sometimes some pages have two numbers: the original sheet number and a stamped number. Check both numbers.

Rolls were listed by county or counties until the 1880 Census, when, with the counties, E.D.s (enumeration districts) begin to appear. Then you would search for the enumeration district within the county and then search for your ancestor.

The partial 1890 schedule only lists counties.

Census Index Books

To find where your ancestor is listed in the population census schedules, start with census index books for the years of 1790-1850. These were privately printed and are available in libraries and other research places. A few states were indexed for 1860 and 1870. The 1900 and 1920 censuses were indexed for all states; the 1910 census is indexed for 21 states. Not all libraries have indexes for every state.

Fig. 13. An 1810 Census Worksheet.

___ 1800 U.S. FEDERAL CENSUS DATE OF SEARCH ___ 18 Feb 1987 ___

XXX 1810 U.S. FEDERAL CENSUS STATE ___ PENNSYLVANIA ___

County	Page No.	Division of County	Name of Head of Household	Males					Females					Other	Slaves
				under 10 yrs.	10-16 years	16-26 years	26-45 years	45 and up	under 10 yrs.	10-16 years	16-26 years	26-45 years	45 and up		
CHES	350	UWCHLAN	Joseph FISHER	0	3	0	0	1	0	1	0	0	1	0	0

62

FEDERAL CENSUS RECORDS

The index books list alphabetically, by line, names just as they are listed in the census, including the county, page number and township. Be aware that some names can be missed. If you can't find the name you are searching for, you may have to go through microfilm of the actual census looking for it.

After finding a name in the census index books, you can then search the census catalogs for the state, county and enumeration district (if available) to find the year and roll numbers by which you can order microfilm through your library or the National Archives.

Information on the Census

For the Federal Population Censuses of 1790 through 1840, only the family heads were listed by name; others in the household were listed by number of free white males by age group, free white females and number of slaves. (See Fig. 13 - 1810.)

In the 1850 through 1880 Federal Population Censuses, each person in the household was listed by name. In each census, increasingly detailed information was posted about each, such as age, occupation, place of birth, years married and home owned or rented. It was noted some persons in the household were not family members, but boarders, servants, relatives, or orphans, etc.

The given information was not always accurate; names were misspelled, people were missed, wrong ages were given.

The 1790-1820 Federal Population Censuses were taken the first Monday in August; the 1830-1850 population census were taken on June 1; the 1910 on April 15 and the 1920 population census was taken on January 1. The date taken will help determine household members' date of birth.

The Soundex System

In 1880, the census was the first indexed according to the Soundex system. At first, only households with a child age 10 or under were listed. In later censuses, all households and individuals were listed, though not all states were indexed. The Soundex listings are in the same catalogs as the Federal Population Census listings, by state and by year.

Fig. 14. Soundex Cards for D. W. Wristen.

U.S. CENSUS FILM T9, R 1328 TAYLOR CO, TX

1880 Soundex Texas (W623) Taylor co (T 773, R 76)

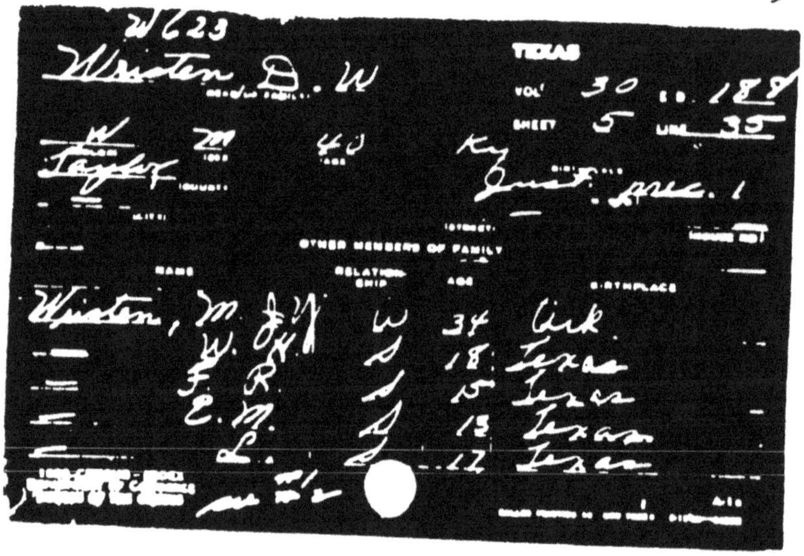

W623
Wristen, D. W — TEXAS
VOL. 30 E.D. 188 SHEET 5 LINE 35
W M 40 Ky
Taylor — Just. prec. 1
OTHER MEMBERS OF FAMILY

NAME	RELATIONSHIP	AGE	BIRTHPLACE
Wristen, M. J.	W	34	Ark
W. H.	S	18	Texas
F. R.	S	15	Texas
E. M.	S	13	Texas
L.	S	12	Texas

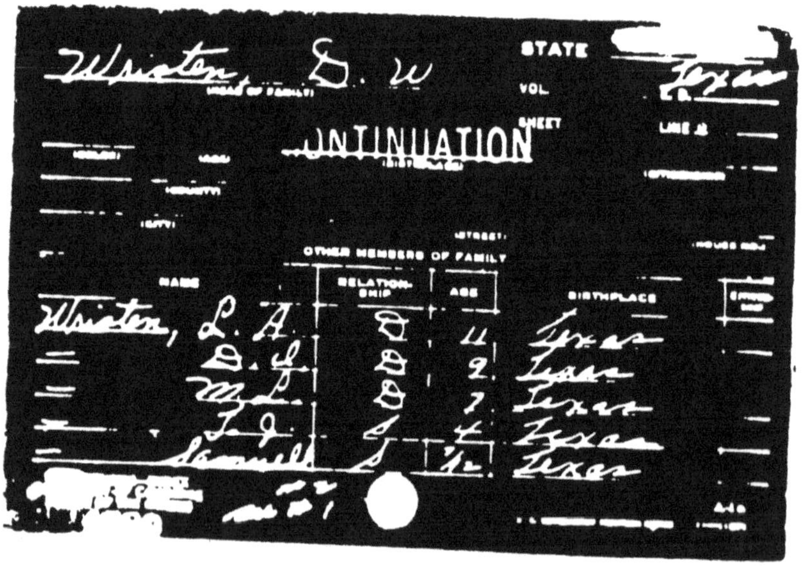

Wristen, D. W — STATE Texas
CONTINUATION
OTHER MEMBERS OF FAMILY

NAME	RELATIONSHIP	AGE	BIRTHPLACE
Wristen, L. A.	D	11	Texas
D. S.	D	9	Texas
M. L.	D	7	Texas
T. J.	S	4	Texas
Samuel	S	1/12	Texas

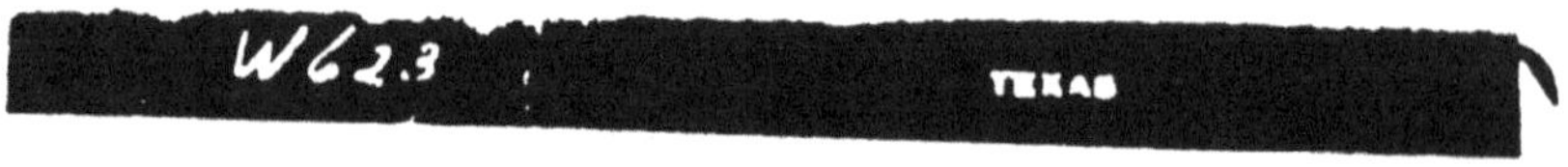

W623 — TEXAS

Fig. 15. Census Worksheet from Soundex Information.

T9 Reel 1328

T773 Reel 76 Soundley W28

Census number: Vol 30, ED 188, Sheet 5, Line 35

1880 Census—United States

State: TEXAS County: TAYLOR Town, Township: JUST. PREC. 1

Dwelling number	Family number	Names	Color/Sex	Age	Relationship to head of house	Single	Married	Widowed	Divorced	Married in census year	Occupation	Other information	Can't read or write	Place of birth	Place of birth of father	Place of birth of mother	Enumerator's date
X73	89	WRISTEN, D. W.	W M 40				1				MERCHANT			KENTUCKY	KENTUCKY	KENTUCKY	1 JUN 1880
		M.Y. (M.J.) (MA MCNAY) W.H.	F 39		WIFE						KEEPING HOUSE			ARKANS			ARKANSAS
		F.R.		18	SON						FARMING			TEXAS	KENTUCKY	"	"
		E.M.		15	SON						FARMING			"	"	"	"
		L.		13	SON						FARMING			"	"	"	"
		L.A.		17	SON						FARMING			"	"	"	"
		D.I.		11	DAUGHTER									"	"	"	"
		M.L.		9	"												
		T.J. or Y.		7	"									"	"	"	"
				4	SON									"	"	"	"
		SAMUEL		7/12	SON									"	"	"	"

65

FEDERAL CENSUS RECORDS

The Soundex is a system of coded 3" x 5" index cards. They are arranged by sound rather than spelling and filmed in vertical rows on microfilm. This system was developed to find names that were recorded under different spellings.

The Bureau of the Census used two separate Soundex cards, one for the head of the household and his family and one for an individual, someone that is enumerated with a family.

The family card shows the head of the family's birthplace, color and age. Other members of the family are listed by name, relationship, age, birthplace and citizenship. At the top of the card is listed the Volume, Enumeration District, Sheet and Line this family would be found on.

The individual card shows the person, who he was enumerated with, the relationship to above and remarks. Other information is the same as for the head of the family and location on the census roll is shown.

Within surnames, the cards are arranged by given name. If there are many Fishers, for instance, they will all be together, but the first names will be alphabetized.

This is a brief explanation of the Soundex Coding Guide.

1 = B P F V
2 = C S K G J Q X Z
3 = D T
4 = L
5 = M N
6 = R

Disregard the letters A, E, I, O, U, W, Y and H which are not coded.

Use the first letter of the surname, which is also not coded. Then use the numbers corresponding to letters. The code must be a three-digit number. Give numbers to the next three consonants of the surname after the first letter. Use zeroes if you run out of letters.

For example, FISHER would be F260. The first letter is F. The I is not counted. The letter S is number 2. H is disregarded as is E. R is number 6. So FISHER = F260.

66

FEDERAL CENSUS RECORDS

A more detailed explanation is in all catalogs listing the Soundex indexes and in many how-to books.

The Census Form or Worksheet

A census form or worksheet is available for each year of the census, identical to the actual census sheet. On this form, extracted information can be copied from the microfilm, such as surname, volume number, enumeration district, etc.

Copy every surname similar to the one you are searching, since misspellings were common. Also, copy names before and after, because censuses were taken down the street, one house after another. When families migrated, it was in groups for safety or because they were related. When they moved into an area, they usually lived near each other, so relatives might be neighbors.

These forms or worksheets are available from genealogical societies, Family History Center Libraries and from commercial sellers, such as Everton Publishers in Logan, Utah, 84321.

Other Federal Census Schedules

There are special schedules for agriculture (1850-80), industry (1850-70), manufacturing (1880); slave schedules, the 1840 census of Revolutionary War pensioners and others.

Mortality schedules for 1850-1885 list deaths in the year of census. They include name, age, sex, state of birth, month of death and cause of death.

These schedules are available through the National Archives.

Ordering Census Microfilm

You can order census microfilm through your library, the Family History Library of the Latter Day Saints Church or from the National Archives.

When you find a surname in the population census index book, along with the county and page it is listed on, look in the Federal Population Census Catalog to find the numbers of the state and roll of microfilm.

Fig. 16. Page from the 1850 South Carolina Census Population Schedule.

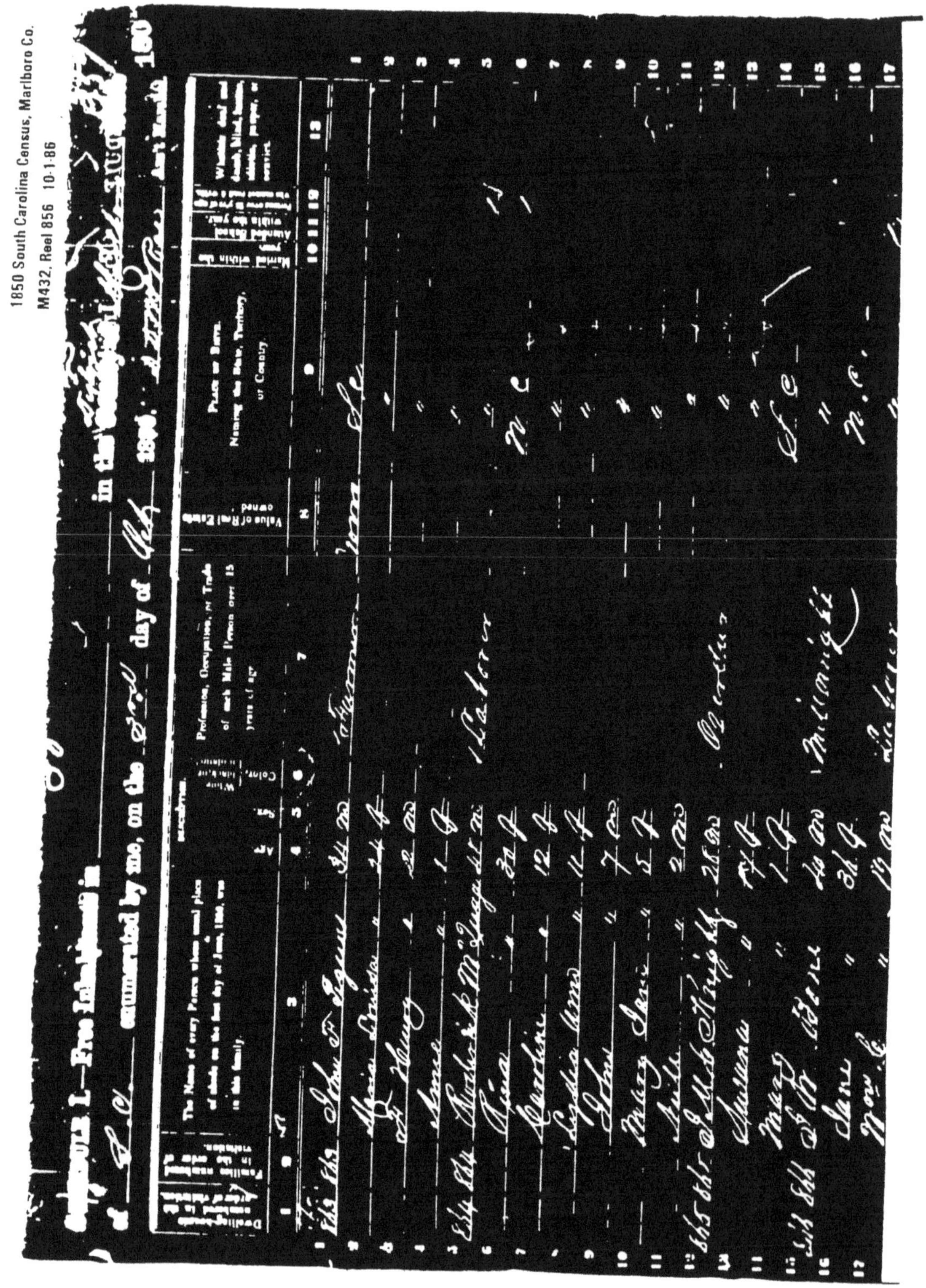

Fig. 17. An 1850 Census Worksheet Showing Information on J. M. C. Knight.

Page	Dwelling number	Family number	Names	Age	Sex	Color	Occupation etc	Value – Real estate	Birthplace	Married within year	School within year	Cannot read or write	Enumeration date	Cal number	Remarks
359	848	848	J MC KNIGHT	28	M		OVERSEER		N. CAROLINA						
			SUSANG	17	F				N CAROLINA						
			MARY	1	F				S.C. Carolina						

State: SOUTH CAROLINA County: MARLBORO (DISTRICT)

1850 Census—United States

Fig. 18. Compilation of Information on Censuses for D. W. Wristen from 1840 to 1920

CENSUS CHART

NAME: Daniel Webster WRISTEN (1839-1918)

(bought land 1868-Texas) T773 R76 Soundex W623

Census Year 1840	Census Year 1850	Census Year 1860	Census Year 1870	Census Year 1880
State Kentucky	State Kentucky	State ___	State Texas	State Texas
County Hopkins	County Muhlenberg	County ___	County Parker	County Taylor
Twp ___	Twp ___	Twp ___	Twp ___	Twp ___
P.O. ___	P.O. ___	P.O. ___	P.O. Ft Worth	P.O. ___
Roll/Page M704, R116 p.288	Roll/Page M432 B 214 Page 191	Roll/Page ___	Roll/Page M593 R1601 P.415, line 19, house 533	Roll/Page T9, R1328 ED188, p 273
List Residents:	List Residents:	List Residents:	List Residents:	List Residents:
Elijah RISTON (33)	Elijah RISTON VA (43)		D. W. Wristen (30)	D. W. WRISTEN KY (40)
Leesy (24)	Leesy (died 1850) KY (34)		M.J. (26)	M. J. (Mary Jane) AR (34)
Martha (6)	Martha A KY (16)		Henry (8)	W. H. (Wm.Henry) KY (18)
Margaret (3)	Margaret E. KY (13)		Frank (6)	F. R. (Frank R.) KY (15)
*Dan (1)	*Dan W. KY (10)		Edward (4)	E. H. (Edward) KY (13)
	William KY (8)		Lee (2 or 4)	L. (Lee A.) KY (17)
Listed on census as:	Francis A. KY (6)		(Girl?) (2/12)	L. A. (Laura A.) KY (11)
1 Male 30-40	John W. KY (4)			D. I. (Dilluly) KY (9)
1 Female 20-30	Mary J. KY (2)			M. L. (Mattie) KY (7)
1 Female 5-10	Rufus G. KY (3/12)			T. J. (Thomas) KY (4)
1 Female Under 5				Samuel KY (4/12)
2 Males under 5				This is the order these names were on census sheet.
(don't know other male)				

CENSUS CHART

NAME: Daniel Webster WRISTEN (1839-1918)

Soundex W623 T1073, B280, 282

Census Year 1890	Census Year 1900	Census Year 1910	Census Year 1920	Census Year ___
State ___	State Texas	State ___	State ___	State ___
County Census	County Callahan	County ___	County ___	County ___
Twp Destroyed	Twp ___	Twp ___	Twp ___	Twp ___
P.O. ___	P.O. ___	P.O. ___	P.O. ___	P.O. ___
Roll/Page ___	Roll/Page T623 B 1617 p.6337	Roll/Page ___	Roll/Page ___	Roll/Page ___
List Residents:	List Residents:	List Residents:	List Residents:	List Residents:
WRISTEN, D.W. (50)	WRISTEN, D.W. KY (60)		D. W. WRISTEN died	
	M.J. AR (54) Died 1900.	Died 1900.	Sept. 16, 1918 (79)	
Susan E. died 1883	William Henry TX (30)			
not found on any census.	Francis TX (35)			
	Edward TX (33)			
Not Listed, but would be this age	L. (Lee A.-died 1883)			
	L.A. (Laura) TX (31)			
	D.I. (Dilluly) TX (29)			
	M.L. (Mattie) TX (27)			
	T.J. (Thomas) TX (24)			
	Samuel TX (20)			
	Charley TX (16)			
	Beulah TX (16)			
	(son-in-law) Frank Conner KY (22)			
	(grandaughter) Ida TX (6)			

70

The rolls may be in the library or they will send away for them. When you get them, you can look at them on one of the readers or reader-printers there. You can print out a copy of the sheet you want or copy it on a census form for that year.

To order, there are forms to fill out; it usually costs around $3.00 a roll (1996) and takes several weeks to get. You may keep it until you are finished. Some states have a time limit.

The first time I looked up my husband's ancestor, Elhanan Fisher, who we heard was in Illinois, I just picked up one of the rolls that the library had for Illinois in 1850 and started to go through name by name. I found Abraham Lincoln in Springfield County, but no Elhanan. After several more searches and many many more hours, I discovered Elhanan and wife and children in Carroll County.

It was only later that I discovered it is possible to get indexes of censuses by state so you can look up your ancestor's name directly, the county he was in and the page he is on, without going though the whole roll.

I started out copying pages of census microfilm on the reader/printer at the library, then reducing, pasting together, copying again, so the page would fit into my census book. Some of it was very hard to read. When I discovered at a seminar that there are forms to copy this information on and to note where it was on the microfilm if you have to look it up again, or if someone else wanted to refer to it, it became much easier.

Now I only copy some originals for reference.

Census Log Sheets

I enter all the census rolls I order on a census log sheet, noting when I ordered, for whom, what state, county and city, the result, when I returned them, and the cost.

I keep copies of state indexes by year in a binder; then I keep census sheets copied on the reader-printer or by hand for each person behind the indexes for the area they are from. I made up summary sheets for each person with all the census years in which they appeared on them. (see Figure 18.)

FEDERAL CENSUS RECORDS

As you follow the census data over the years, you can see families start and grow, children marry and scatter, the areas the family traveled through if they migrated to new areas, what they owned, and where they ended up.

To Sum Up:

1. Catalogs of Federal Population Census Schedules available on microfilm are at libraries or archives, or can be ordered from the National Archives for a nominal fee.

2. Soundex lists are included in these catalogs. These are coded last-name indexes based on the way a name sounds and not how it is spelled.

3. There are special agricultural, industrial, manufacturing and mortality census schedules, as well as others, available from the National Archives.

4. There are name index books for almost every state with surnames in alphabetical order.

5. Copy every surname like the one you are looking for. Note who their neighbors were.

6. Use census forms or worksheets to copy data from microfilm.

7. Keep a record of census records ordered, for whom and where, and cost of rolls, census forms, and copying.

CHAPTER 9

CHURCH RECORDS, CEMETERIES AND OBITUARIES

CHURCH RECORDS

Search church records for birth, christening, baptism, marriage, death and burial records. If you know the church, you may go there directly. Otherwise, church records and indexes are available in some libraries and archives.

I was not successful in finding many church records, except Quaker records, and very old Church of England records, in spite of much correspondence; however, I did find indexes. It is hard to find where churches have sent their records or which records they kept or if they still have them.

Quaker records showed marriage certificates with lists of all attendees. Their Monthly Meeting Minutes showed transfers to other monthly meetings, marriage requests and many other occasions and happenings.

Many books and indexes have been written, containing records of Monthly Meetings, marriages, etc. I liked Encyclopedia of American Quaker Genealogy by William Wade Hinshaw, ed. These books and indexes can be seen at libraries and at locations such as the Swarthmore College in Swarthmore, Pennsylvania. I have written to Swarthmore College requesting searches on ancestors, and was sent quite lengthy letters with much information.

The Maryland State Archives has lists of christenings, births and marriages, etc for various churches in the area, like St. John's at Broad Creek in Piscataway, Prince George's County and All Hallows Episcopal Church in Anne Arundel County.

Historical societies may have church membership registers and bible records.

Each state archives keeps the oldest records; it is the newest records that are the hardest to find.

CEMETERIES

Cemeteries and funeral homes are noted on death certificates.

You could contact the funeral director listed on the death certificate who would have records on the cemetery. Sometimes, they will send you a copy of the obituary. Funeral directors may have information that wasn't published in the obituary.

If you are not sure where the burial place is, county offices have listings of cemeteries; some are on family property, others are government-owned or private, owned by an association in the township. Some churches have the cemetery in the churchyard.

Some areas have cemetery associations associated with historical societies.

It is hard to find church cemetery records, especially very old ones. Sometimes, state archives have them; other times, the church libraries have them. But sometimes they have not been kept.

The county or township office may have maps of where cemeteries are located. If you know the cemetery, you may write care of the sexton. If you go in person, inquire at the county office, where you could find the sexton or caretaker of the cemetery. They would have plat maps and lists of where individuals are buried.

The sextons and caretakers we talked to were very helpful and took as much time as necessary to look up the grave and then took us to see the grave. Some of them kept the records at their house and they took us there to go through them. Other times the records are kept on the premises of the cemetery.

The sexton usually records who bought the lot or lots. Also, we found purchase of cemetery lots in grantor-grantee deed books.

Bear in mind, though, that you may not find records of some cemeteries or there will be incomplete records.

When you are in the town your ancestor was buried in, it would be helpful to check the telephone directory for living relative by that surname. We did so and were rewarded by meeting a very nice group of people, who talked to us about old family stories and loaned us some great photographs.

Searching Cemeteries

When you go to search cemeteries, wear long pants and sturdy shoes as much walking may be involved in mud and in tall grass. I was told there may be snakes in the grass.

Take a camera to photograph the grave or graves you hope to find.

In some cemeteries, some tombstones have been broken and may be piled up in a corner. On very old tombstones, the writing has disintegrated from the weather. They are usually at the very back of cemeteries and in much disrepair.

Occasionally, all the early stones are gone and the only records are sparse and kept at State Archives, as we found at the St. Paul's at Baden Church in southern Maryland.

At the Grave or Family Plot

Draw a layout of the grave, its location in reference to the entrance of the cemetery and the road it is on. If it is a family plot, draw all the graves and the names and dates. Note the wording or legend on each, and the type of carving. You may find a pair of hands, an open book, angels or other. Civil War veterans may have a metal cross by their grave.

Look at each stone. Sometimes maiden names are inscribed. There may be birth and death dates of babies who died young and no other record may be available. You may find persons of whom no other record has remained.

Errors can be made on the tombstone if it is put up some time after the death, so this information needs to be verified.

You may try your hand at making rubbings of the tombstone by placing paper over the printing and rubbing with a crayon or charcoal. Be careful not to erase anything or damage it.

75

Look at all the stones at the cemetery, if it is small. Sometimes a related family group might be nearby or other members of the family are buried there.

If the cemetery is large, check the sexton's records for members of your family.

Many genealogical societies publish books of cemetery indexes and inscriptions as do historical societies and other groups. These can be purchased from the societies or found in libraries.

OBITUARIES

Obituaries usually can be found in local newspapers and in old newspapers on microfilm. Some libraries have indexed their obituaries; but otherwise, you will have to read through all the papers in your time period.

You can write to the library in the county where your ancestor died, asking if they keep records of obituaries. You can also write to genealogical or historical societies in that area; they keep many local records as do some university libraries.

Sometimes, obituaries are very brief with date of death, age, location of services and cemetery. Other times, they are lengthy with birthplace, parents, survivors, places lived, organizations belonged to, schools, degrees, military service, places worked, and church and community service information. Sometimes, the facts are not correct as the person giving them may be misinformed on some data.

In our town, obituaries are submitted from the funeral home. If the person is very elderly with few relatives or friends, the family may not put an obituary in the paper.

Some places have very brief paid death notices.

As you go through newspapers in search of obituaries and articles about your ancestor, stop and read some of the other articles and notices to get a flavor of the times.

At times, besides the obituary, an article is written, with more information if the person was rather prominent.

We found in the county where my husband's ancestor died, the funeral director took information from people and composed the obituary to be put in the paper. We asked for information from him and found that sometimes he doesn't put all the information given into the obituary, but keeps a fact sheet. He gave us a copy of the original data, since my husband was a relative. So perhaps you could inquire after that.

In my husband's great-great-grandfather's case, there were obituaries, articles and photographs in several papers in Abilene where he had been Mayor around the turn of the century. There were also obituaries in papers in the next county, where he lived.

Finding Death Place When Different from Burial Place

My husband's other great-great-grandfather died at his daughter's home in Indiana, but was buried in the family plot in Illinois.

We couldn't find where he died. We found the date of his death (1918) on his tombstone, which we found in Mt. Carroll, Illinois, with the help of the local genealogical society.

We read all the local newspapers around the time of his death. We finally found his obituary, where it was stated that he died out of state in Terre Haute, Indiana. We wrote to the Indiana Record Bureau and did get a copy of the death certificate. The death certificate was issued in Indiana. Death certificates are issued where the death took place, even though the burial may be elsewhere.

If you can't find a death certificate or grave, to approximate a date of death, you may use the sources you have, with several obituaries, articles and local histories, etc. to provide evidence that it is probable that this person died about this time. A question mark or explanation should be used to indicate you don't have a definite date.

To Sum Up:

1. Church records, like membership and parish registers, and indexes, may be found in some historical and genealogical societies, libraries and archives.

2. Genealogical and historical societies compile records by visiting their local cemeteries and listing each grave. These records are published in their bulletins or quarterlies. These compilations are often for sale and in libraries.

3. You may write to the church where your ancestors belonged where records may be found. Sometimes the records have been transferred somewhere else.

4. Death certificates may name cemeteries, funeral homes and churches, as well as other information.

5. County offices have records of where cemeteries are.

6. The sexton or caretaker would have records of where the graves are and who is buried in the cemetery.

7. Draw a layout of the grave or family plot, noting where it is is in relation to entrance. Note all buried there and include all names, dates and inscriptions.

8. Photograph the area if possible.

9. Obituaries may be found in local papers or old papers on microfilm in libraries, etc.

10. Compiled church records, cemetery records and abstracted obituaries are found in many repositories.

CHAPTER 10

LAND RECORDS

1. Land records are probably the earliest records available all the way back to colonial times.

2. Land records can be divided into those created by governments granting land to individuals or groups and those created by selling and buying of land by individuals or groups.

3. There have been many types of land records created.

4. Land is measured by two systems: metes and bounds and the rectangular system.

5. Land records are located in various offices at the federal, state and county level.

6. Land records provide much information about location, relationships, neighbors, occupation.

7. Tax records contain much valuable information.

Early Land Records

At first, England claimed much land. Grants of land were made to the colonies. The colonies granted or sold the land to individuals or groups. They then sold and bought it from each other.

Some early land records were of federal warrants, grants and patents where the colonies granted land to the early settlers.

When a settler desired certain land, an application for a grant was submitted and a warrant was issued for a survey. Then a patent was granted through which title was secured.

Fig. 19. Treasury Warrant.

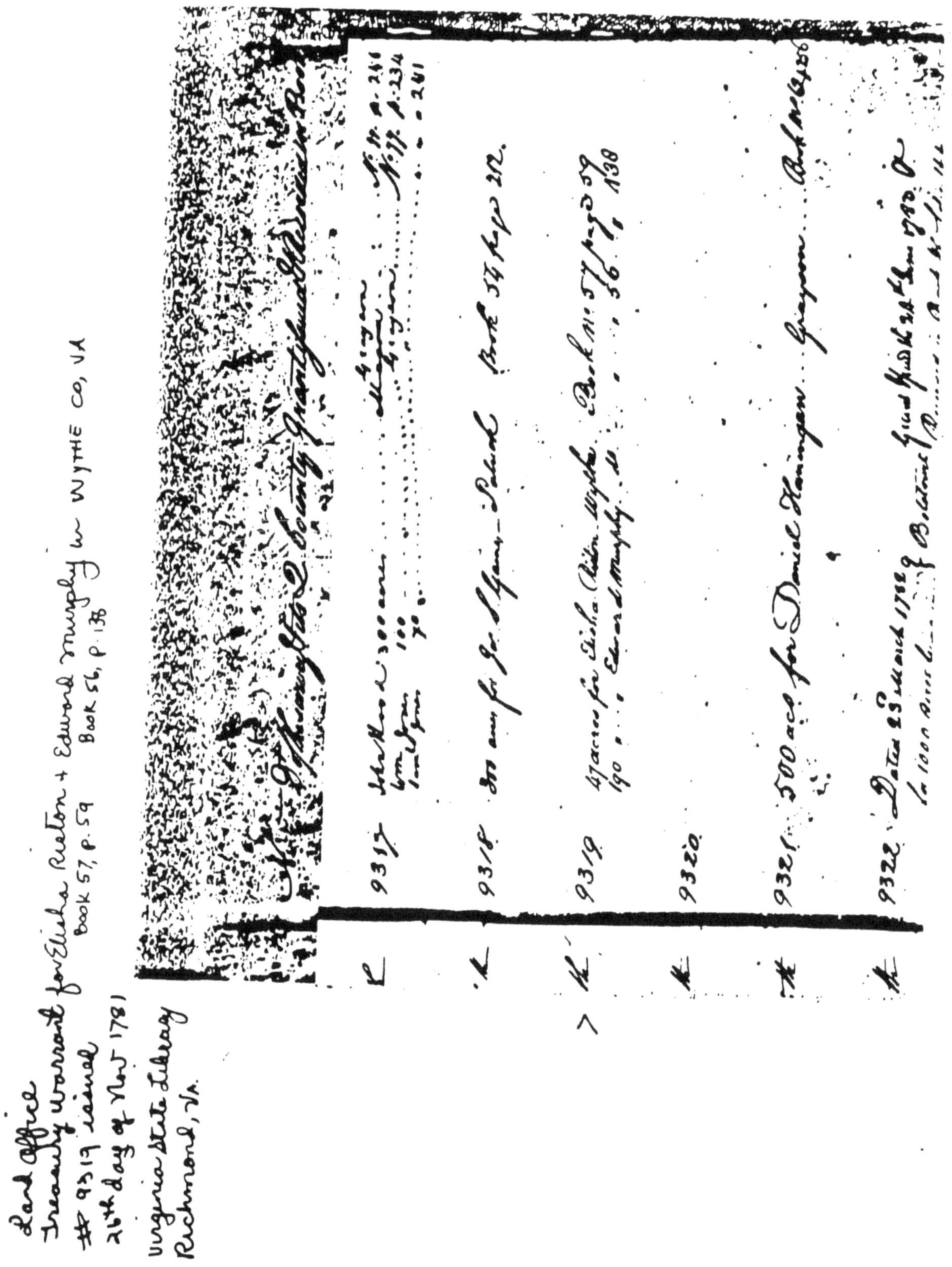

LAND RECORDS

A warrant was official permission to have the land surveyed and a map or plat drawn to produce a legal description.

A patent or grant was a document transferring title to land from a government to a private party after they had the land surveyed and were entitled to have clear title to it through a warrant.

I was fortunate to find a copy of a warrant in Wythe County, West Virginia, dated 1781, (See Fig. 19.) for one of my husband's ancestors, Elisha Riston, by calling the Virginia State Library. The gentleman I talked to found the name and the warrant and mailed me a copy, for which I was very thankful.

I found that after receiving a warrant, the purchaser had to have the land surveyed and had to furnish a chain man (in Virginia) to help with the surveying (to hold the chain when measuring). A chain was 66 feet long, with links of wire. Family tradition was that Elisha's brother, Reason, acted as chain man. This was done in 1805. In 1808, Elisha received Grant #57 along with Edward Murphy. (See Fig. 20.)

Headright Grant

Another way to acquire land was the headright grant, which was paid to those who transported settlers, indentured servants or themselves to the new land--usually 50 acres of land per head.

Indentured servants were committed for a certain term, like four or ten years, or until they were a certain age, after which they were free. This method paid their passage over.

Bounty Land

Bounty land was given to soldiers for military service in the Revolutionary War or any war up to 1855, when the last Bounty Land Act passed. This land could be claimed by widow or heirs.

Sale of Land

Land was also sold by individuals or by land companies.

Fig. 20. Grant #57.

TRANSCRIPTION OF COPY OF THE ORIGINAL GRANT #57
FOR 47 ACRES IN WYTHE COUNTY, VIRGINIA
ISSUED TO ELISHA RISTON PER SURVEY DIRECTED BY
LAND OFFICE TREASURY WARRANT NO. 9319, DATED 26 NOVEMBER 1781
SURVEY DATED 25 FEBRUARY 1805
(REEL 123, PG. 59, 2 MARCH 1808
VIRGINIA STATE LIBRARY, RICHMOND, VIRGINIA 1992)

WILLIAM H. CABELL, ESQUIRE, GOVERNOR OF THE COMMONWEALTH OF VIRGINIA. TO ALL TO WHOM THESE PRESENTS SHALL COME GREETING. KNOW YE, THAT BY VIRTUE OF A LAND OFFICE TREASURY WARRANT, NO. 9319, ISSUED THE 26TH DAY OF NOVEMBER 1781, THERE IS GRANTED BY THE SAID COMMONWEALTH UNTO ELISHA RISTON, A CERTAIN TRACT OR PARCEL OF LAND CONTAINING FORTY-SEVEN ACRES BY SURVEY BEARING DATE THE TWENTY FIFTH DAY OF FEBRUARY, ONE THOUSAND EIGHT HUNDRED AND FIVE LYING AND BEING IN THE COUNTY OF WYTHE, ON THE WATERS OF THE SOUTH FORK OF HOLSTEIN RIVER, AND BOUNDED AS FOLLOWETH TO WIT:

BEGINNING AT A WHITE OAK AND DOUBLE CHESNUT THENCE WITH TWENTY-ONE DEGREES WEST TWENTY-TWO POLES TO A LARGE CHESNUT, CORNER TO THE LAND OF A MATTHEW KINKANNON, THENCE WITH A LINE OF THE SAME, NORTH EIGHTY-FIVE DEGREES, WEST FIFTY-NINE POLES TO A LARGE CHESNUT, NORTH SIXTY-NINE DEGREES, WEST THIRTY-FIVE POLES TO A DOGWOOD IN THE COUNTY LINE AND WITH THE SAME, SOUTH FORTY POLES TO A BLACK OAK, SOUTH TWENTY-EIGHT DEGREES, WEST TWENTY POLES TO A CHESNUT OAK AND GUM, SOUTH TWENTY-SIX DEGREES, EAST SIXTY-FOUR POLES TO A STAKE, AND THENCE NORTH FORTY-EIGHT DEGREES EAST ONE HUNDRED AND SIXTEEN POLES TO THE BEGINNING WITH ITS APPURTENANCES; TO HAVE AND TO HOLD THE SAID TRACT OR PARCEL OF LAND WITH ITS APPURTENANCES TO THE SAID ELISHA RISTON AND HIS HEIRS FOREVER. IN WITNESS WHEREOF THE SAID WILLIAM H. CABELL ESQUIRE, GOVERNOR OF THE COMMONWEALTH OF VIRGINIA HATH HEREUNTO SET HIS HAND AND CAUSED THE LESSER SEAL OF THE SAID COMMONWEALTH TO BE AFFIXED AT RICHMOND ON THE NINTH DAY OF MARCH IN THE YEAR OF OUR LORD ONE THOUSAND EIGHT HUNDRED AND EIGHT AND OF THE COMMONWEALTH THE THIRTY SECOND.

S/ WM. H. CABELL.

LAND RECORDS

Other Land Records

Land transactions between individuals or groups generated other land records, such as deeds, mortgages, indentures, bills of sale, etc.

Measurement of Land

Two systems are used to measure land: Metes and Bounds and the Rectangular System.

Metes and Bounds

Metes is the measurement in degrees. One degree is 1/360th of a circle. Bounds is the distance in feet, rods, chains, etc.

Surveyors used cairns, or piles of stones, as well as trees, etc. at the corners of property. The description was written as starting at the beginning at a known point, then so many degrees north, or whatever direction the land was surveyed, to another point; thence in another direction, until the line was back to the beginning.

The description from the Indenture of 1845 (See Fig. 21.) from Elijah Wristen (Grantor) to William Medlock (Grantee) of 100 acres on the Waters of Flat Creek was used to draw the third land plat in Figure 22.

On Figure 22, three land plats are shown. The top two show the two plots of 50 acres each Elijah Wristen bought in Hopkins County, Kentucky, in 1838 and 1844. The bottom plat shows the 100 acres he sold. This plat shows that the two earlier plats were combined in this 100 acres, which has the same known points. This was surveyed by the metes and bounds system.

By comparing corners and known points, such as the black gum and elm, three black oaks and white oak and gum, you can see that the top two plats comprise the third.

After awhile, trees or other markers, like a stake, might not last, so surveyors would go back and resurvey using more permanent markers.

Fig. 21. Indenture and Transcription.

INDENTURE
8 August 1845, Book 12, Page 172
Hopkins County Courthouse, KY - General Index to Deeds
(Copied and transcribed May 1988)

Elijah Wristen (Grantor) to William Medlock (Grantee)
100 Acres on the Waters of Flat Creek

This indenter made and entred into this the eight day of August in the year of our Lord one thousand, eigt hundred and forty-five (1845) betwene Elijah Wristen of the County of Hopkins and state of Kentucky of the one part and William Medlock of the County and state aforsaid of the other part Witnesseth that the said Wristen for and in consideration of three(?) hundred and fifty dollars to him in hand paid the recpt whereof he hereby acnolledges haith granted, bargend and sold and by these present doath grant, bairgen, sel and convey unto the said Medlock, his airs and assigns forever a certain tract of land cituated lying and beaing in the County of Hopkins and stait aforesaid on the waters of flat creak containg by servey one hundred acres and bounded as follows to wit-Beginning at a black oak on the bank of a brainch, runing North 75 E 186 poals (poles) to a wight oak and gum thence South 107 pols to three black oaks thence S 75 W 144 pols to a double popler on the bank of said branch thence with the sevrel miandrs of said branch to the Bgining with all its appurtanances thairunto belonging or in any wise apperteaining to to haive and to hoald the land hearby conveaded unto the said Medlock, his hears and asins forever and the said Wristen, his airs and asins the said tract of land with its appertiances unto the said Medlock his ars and asins aganest the lofel (lawful) claims or clames of all and ever person or persons whatsomever doth and will warant and forever defend by thes presents. In telamonity whareof the said Wristen haith hearunto subscribed his naime and afixed his seail the day and daight (date) above writen.

Elijah Wristen (his seal)

Test Ebenezer B. Sisk
        Martin Sisk
Kentucky
Hopkins County   (Seal Sct)

This Indenture was this day produced to me by Elijah Wristen the grantor therein named and acknowledged by him to be his act and deed.

In Testimony whereof and that the said Indenture and this certificate are truly recorded in my office, I have hereunto subscribed my name the 23d day of May 1846.
Sam Woodson C.H.C.C.
By Sam c. Woodson D.C.

Fig. 22. Land Plats.

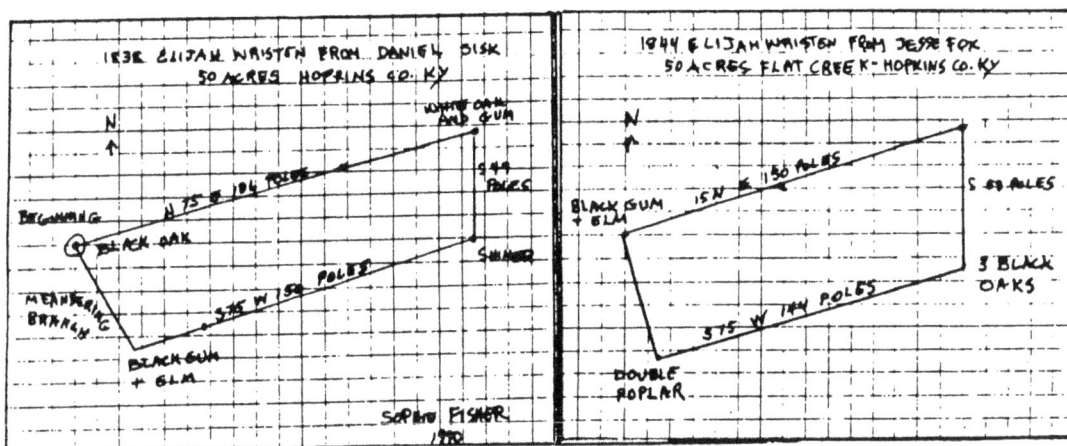

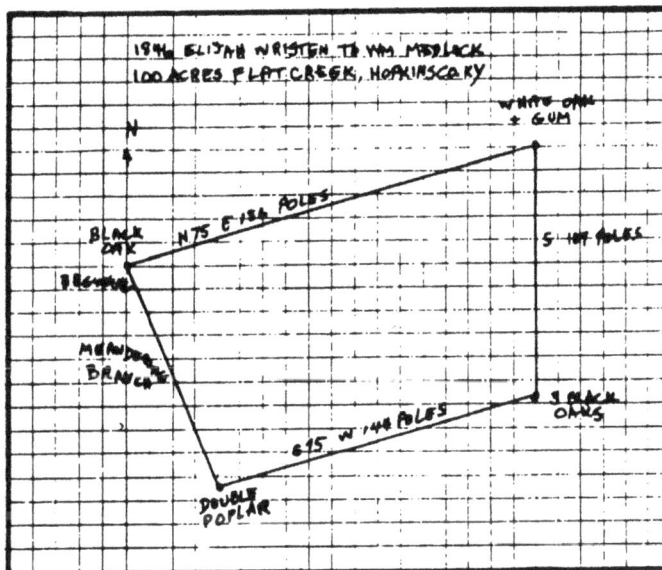

Fig. 23. Rectangular System of Surveying

6	5	4	3	2	1
7	8	9	10	11	12
18	17	16	15	14	13
19	20	21	22	23	24
30	29	28	27	26	25
31	32	33	34	35	36

*Each township is divided into 36 sections of 640 acres,
one square mile each. This township is located in Township 3 North,
Range 3 West or T3N-R3W. It is 3 townships north of the base line
and 3 townships west of the meridian.*

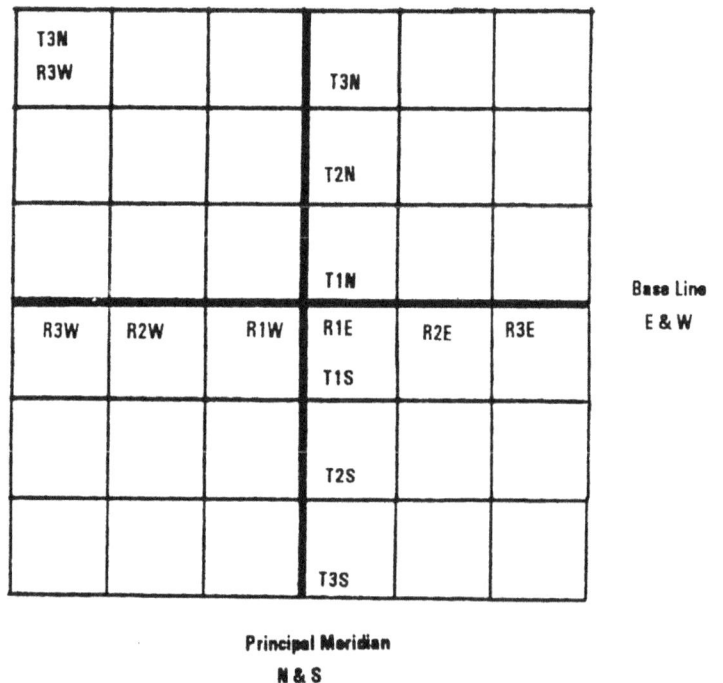

T3N R3W			T3N		
			T2N		
			T1N		Base Line E & W
R3W	R2W	R1W	R1E / T1S	R2E	R3E
			T2S		
			T3S		

Principal Meridian
N & S

Base Line and Principal Meridian Intersect.

LAND RECORDS

Later, benchmarks replaced old landmarks. Benchmarks were small cement markers, with the description etched in brass attached to the top, which were placed at the corners of the property. Surveys were then made from benchmarks.

State-Land States and the Public Domain

The 13 original states plus Kentucky, Maine, Tennessee, Texas, Vermont and West Virginia (which was formed from part of Virginia) were called state-land states and continued to grant land as before the Revolution.

The rest of the land was called public land or the public domain, from which the the 30 public-land states were formed.

In 1785, the federal government decreed that the public domain land be surveyed using a rectangular survey system.

The Rectangular System

The Northwest Ordinance of 1785 provided that the public domain would be laid out rectangularly in townships and sections. The Rectangular System of Surveys consisted of a base line running east and west and a principal meridian running north and south. Each state had its own base line and meridian which started at a specific spot in the state, usually in the state capital.

Townships east of the meridian are numbered Range 1 East, Range 2 East, etc. to the eastern boundary of the state. Those townships west of the meridian are numbered Range 1 West, Range 2 West, to the western boundary To further identify the location of each township either north or south of the base line, they are numbered Township 1 North, Township 2 North, etc. and part of the legal description of each parcel of land within the boundaries of the state contain the township description, such as T7N-R6E which locates the township as being 7 Townships North of the base line and 6 Townships East of the Principal Meridian.

The townships were to be six miles square and divided in 36 sections of 640 acres, 1 square mile each, numbered from 1 to 36, in serpentine fashion, back and forth, beginning in the upper right-hand corner.

Fig. 24. Grantee-Grantor Index.

GRANTEE INDEX TO DEEDS, ANSON COUNTY, N. C.

GRANTEES Family Name	GIVEN NAMES ABCDEFGH	GIVEN NAMES IJKLMNO	GIVEN NAMES PQRSTUVWXYZ	GRANTORS	DATE	Kind of Instrument	Book	Page	WHERE LOCATED
Womble	Henry			State of N C	Aug 18 1825	Grant	W	10	Adj Jesse Melton
do	Henry			Geo Duren	Sept 25 1819	Deed	W	60	Little Brown Creek
do	Henry			David Diggs	Sept 17 1825	Deed	W	61	Adj Jas Kimberly
do	Henry			Hardy Ogvin	Mar 29 1823	Deed	X	45	Brown Creek
do	Henry			David Gaddy	June 3 1836	Deed	Z	477	Adj Womble
do	Henry			Jas F Cason	Feb 5 1851	Deed	13	512	Brown Creek
do	Henry			Henry Womble Est By Comr	May 27 1857	Dower	15	317	Brown Creek
do		Jane		Hampton Huntley & wife	Apr 26 1873	Deed	19	39	Brown Creek
do	Geo W								

LAND RECORDS

The sections are divided into quarters of 160 acres each and are identified as NW Quarter Section, NE Quarter Section, etc. Sections divided further would be described as the NE 1/4 of the NE 1/4 of the SW 1/4 of Sec. 17, T7N-R6E.

The rectangular system was used in platted land. Any land not platted, like large farms, was surveyed by metes and bounds. Combinations of the two systems were used when land consisted of a platted lot and a parcel of land outside the plat.

If you find a description in an index or an old deed, you can go to the assessor's office in the township to get help in finding the location of the land.

Location of Land Records

Some land records are at the county court house. They may also be at the courthouse of the parent county from which the county you are searching was formed. This office is known as the Registrar of Deeds, County Recorder, Clerk of the Circuit Court or other designation.

Grantor-Grantee Indexes

Deeds and other land documents are listed in Grantor (seller)--Grantee (buyer) indexes. They are kept in ledgers at the county court house. They are listed by surname, though not alphabetically, under letters of the alphabet, They are entered by year and date; many ledgers date back to the start of a county.

These land documents may be recorded some years after they are written and dated.

The information in the grantor-grantee indexes is date of record, names of grantor-grantee, the instrument, such as patent, grant, deed, warranty, mortgage, etc., description, volume number and page number (See Fig. 24.)

To Search for Land of Your Ancestors

At the courthouse, you will be shown where the indexes and deedbooks are and you can take them down one by one to search the indexes and then the deeds.

Fig. 25. Abstract of A Deed.

ABSTRACT OF DEED

Compiler ___SOPHIE FISHER___ Surname ___FISHER, THOMAS (SR)___

Address ___5423 S. DYEWOOD___ Date Abstracted ___25 SEPT 1992___

___FLINT MI 48532___

County ___CHESTER___ State ___PA___ (Kennett Twp)

Deed Book ___PATENT BOOK A, VOL 10___ Pages ___43, 44, 45___

Repository ___PA HISTORICAL + MUSEUM COMM. DIV OF LAND REC. BOX 1026___
___HARRISBURG, PA 17108-1026___

Grantor(s) ___JOHN PENN, THOMAS PENN +___ Residence ___- PROPRIETARIES - PROVINCE___
___RICHARD PENN, ESQ___
___OF PENNSYLVANIA + COS OF NEW CASTLE, KENT + SUSSEX ON DELAWARE___

Grantee(s) ___THOMAS FISHER___ Residence ___CHESTER CO. PA___
___KENNETT TWSP___

Date of Deed ___16 JAN 1739___ Date Recorded ___16 MAR 1739/40___
___mail every year (out rent)___

Consideration ___80 POUNDS 13 SHILLINGS   199½A plus___
___+ 6a allowance   2 silver shillings English.___

Signature(s) or Mark(s) ___mark   X___

Witnesses ___Thomas Penn___

Description ___199½ acres + 6 acres allowance for roads + Hwy.___
___Beginning at a Post at corner of WM WEBBS Land___
___NW 119 perches to white oak by WM Webbs and___
___Zorobabel THATCHERS LAND NE ¼ N 242 perches___
___to Post by lands of EZEKIAL HARLAN + ABRAHAM___
___PARKER SE 166½ PERCHES TO POST BY___
___SARAH HARLAN, SW 237 perches to beginning___

___Perch same as Pole or Rod = 25 links 100 links (or 4 poles)___
___= 1 chain 80 chains (800 links) = 1 mile___

Other Pertinent Information ___Warrant #49 under name of Thomas Robinson + Thomas___
___Fisher___

Release of Dower _____

90

LAND RECORDS

Copy all entries for surnames you are searching from both grantor and grantee indexes for at least 10-15 years or from the first surname you find to the last.

If you find grantor entries for your surnames, try to find the grantee entries.

When you find the surnames, see the volume and page number of the deeds or other instruments. Then go to those volumes of the ledgers for copies of the deeds you found indexed.

If you would like a copy of a deed or other document you find, someone will take the ledger and make a copy for you for the small cost of copying. This was the procedure at the county courthouses we went to; other counties may have other procedures.

After you have a copy made, write a citation for it: where and when you found it, what courthouse you found it in, the date, all the pertinent information. Be sure to get the legal description of where the land is located.

When you get it home, transcribe the deed as best as you can, especially when it is old, faded and very hard to read.

Other Locations

Indexes, handwritten copies and microfilm of early land records can also be found at state archives, state land offices, Bureaus of Land Management,the LDS Family History Centers and at the National Archives. However, the National Archives only has records for the 30 public land states.

Abstracts of deeds and other land documents are in book form in libraries and archives. An abstract is a short summary of a document, with all pertinent facts and dates noted. You can make abstracts of the land documents you find. (See Fig. 25.)

Below are some examples of land documents I found and how different states keep records:

In Pennsylvania

For example, in the Commonwealth of Pennsylvania, the Pennsylvania State Archives at Harrisburg, Pennsylvania, will make a record search for an application, warrant, survey, and patent for early settlers. The order form can be sent for; the fees are noted for each search. When you learn volume and page numbers from the search, you can order copies of documents.

In correspondence with the State Archives at Harrisburg, Pennsylvania (1993), I was advised that state land records documenting the sales of land by the Proprietary (in colonial times) and the Commonwealth (after the Revolution) governments were maintained by that office. Searches are done only for original records.

I was fortunate to have found through this search a patent to Thomas Fisher in Kennett, Chester County, dated 16 January 1739/1740 from the sons of William Penn: John, Thomas and Richard Penn, Esquires, for 199 1/2 acres + 6 acres allowance for roads and highways, in Patent Book A, Volume 10, pages 43, 44, and 45.

Land records in some states are at Land Offices.

In Texas

In another example, from my experience, in Texas, there is the Texas General Land Office which you can visit or write to, where they keep records of Spanish and Mexican land grants, headrights, pre-emption grants or homestead or settler's claims, bounty and donation grants, school land sales, patents, deeds, etc.

My husband's ancestor, Daniel W. Wristen, settled in 1864 on 160 acres of vacant land on the South Fork of Spring Creek, a tributary of the Brazos River, and improved it for three years, per the Homestead Act of 1862.

Fig. 26. Corrected Field Notes.

Elijah Wriston's 160 Acres in Weatherford (1858) Corrected Field Notes, File No. Robertson-3-4379, Book 1, p. 205; (1887) Premption Book A, p. 250. (General Land Office, Austin, TX)

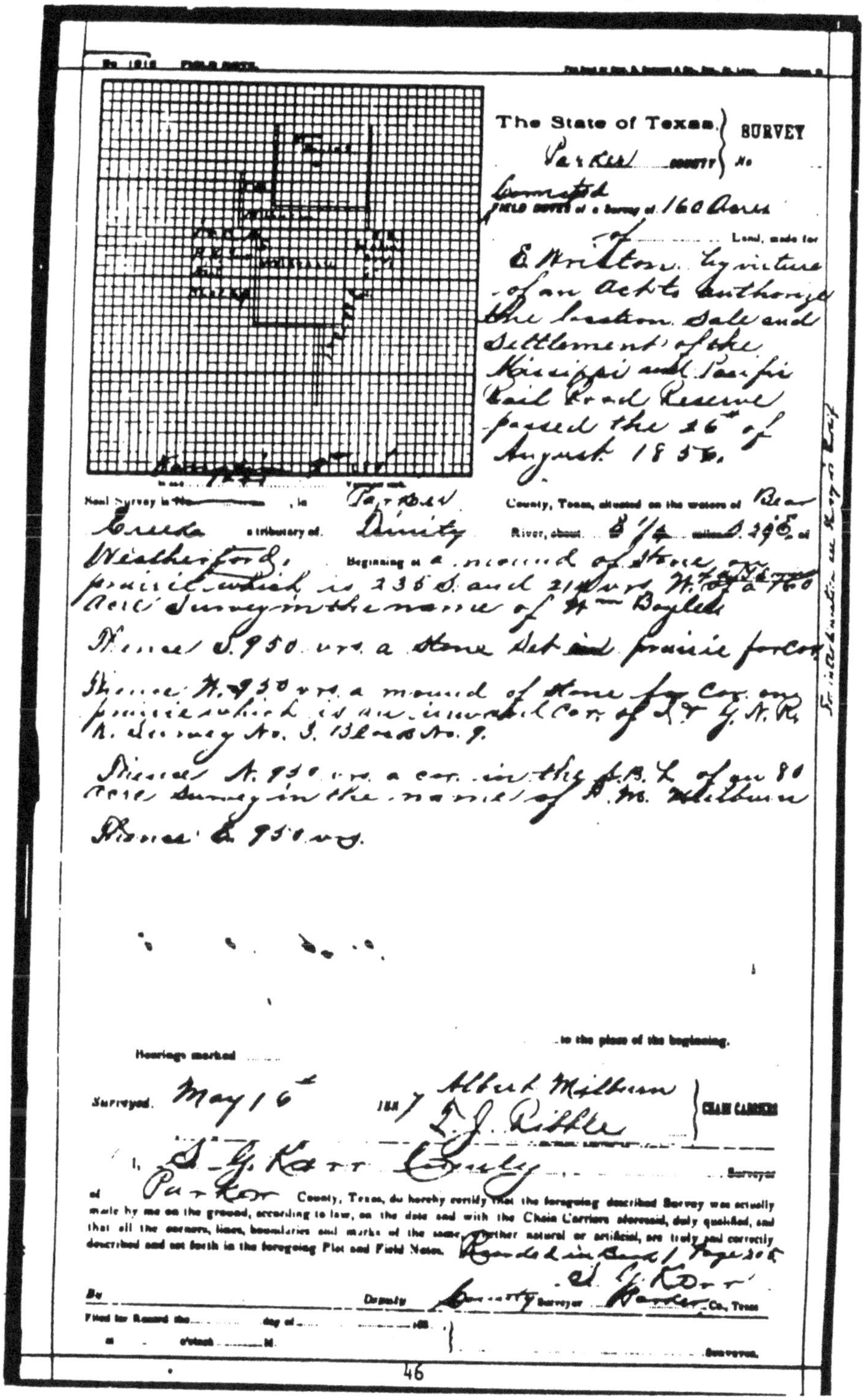

LAND RECORDS

Field notes at the Texas General Land Office at Austin, Texas, (See Fig.26) show the survey and the Affidavit of Settlement, per a pre-emption grant that gave the land as a gift to three-year settlers. The final title was issued under a Patent.

As land was sold or granted, many variations in the provisions or requirements of recipients were enacted over the years.

Land Records Provide Much Information

These various documents show who bought and sold land, relationships, residence of grantor (seller) and grantee (buyer), previous owners, the location of property, rivers and streams nearby, acreage, neighbors on all sides, who might be related or who have daughters or sons who married into the family, signatures of grantor and grantee, and witnesses.

You can find where your ancestor lived, when he bought property and when he sold it, when he came to and left a particular location. Then you have to find where he went next, checking adjoining areas.

Census returns might show you where he located. Other documents such as marriage records, court records or death records might have a clue.

Land records show what land was purchased and deeded for cemetery lots, was given to what persons, what land was left to beneficiaries, what land was resurveyed, and other transactions.

But the most important reason to locate all land records pertaining to your ancestor is to show where he was at different points in time.

Beyond Basic Land Research

Seeking Grantor-Grantee records is not too hard. Seeking further land records is a very involved process. You have to know about the each state and what measuring methods they used and then what methods were used later, with various technical details.

LAND RECORDS

Further Information on Land Records

More detailed information on all of the above can be found in
The Source under Chapter 7, Land and Tax Records, which also
has a section for each state, with a history of their land
records, much description of where to find them and suggested
readings.

A very good write-up is in In Search of Family History: A
Starting Place by Paul Drake, J.D. by Heritage Books, Inc.

Many guides to seeking land records have been issued by states
and by individuals and are available in libraries, bookstores,
etc. Many archives have listings of all the records they have.

Tax Records

Tax records are for real property, personal property or both.
I believe tax records are the most consistent, as every person
pays some kind of taxes.

Tax records are not too easy to find in courthouses or the
county offices. Some tax assessors only keep the latest tax
records and the rest are stored in inaccessible places or
destroyed, as we found.

Copies of older tax records and assessments are found in the
state archives or state library. In some states, like
Maryland, there are tax assessment books by districts on
microfilm. There are also equity, debt, and tax sale books.

Some tax lists were microfilmed by the LDS Library. Some have
been published in index books. Books and articles have been
published on compiled tax lists. There is a lot of reference
material available, but it takes time to find it.

I did find volumes listing personal property tax lists at a
state archive, but not any record of the same person owning
property. I learned a person did not need to own property to
be taxed on his personal property, such as slaves, horses, and
cattle. Personal property tax lists can establish where the
ancestor was at this particular time and so are helpful.

LAND RECORDS

I've only skimmed the surface of this subject and wanted merely to let you know about some of the different methods of survey and disposal of land.

To Sum Up:

1. There are many types of land records, from very early to present day.

2. Research is needed to find where to locate land records, as they are kept in various places.

3. Land is measured by metes and bounds and a rectangular system.

4. Tax records may show where and when a taxpayer lived in an area, when he died and other information.

5. Books and articles have been published on compiled tax records.

6. Personal property taxes can be levied even though no real property is owned and can pinpoint where and when a person lived in the area.

7. To find land, you need a legal description of where the land is located; then qualified persons in government offices can help you.

CHAPTER 11

RESEARCH AWAY FROM HOME

1. If your ancestors were from another area, discover the counties and states and towns where your ancestors lived. You may find this from vital record indexes, census indexes, etc.

2. Some counties were formed from other counties, so check The Handy Book.

3. Go to or write to the county clerks in the states where you believe your ancestors were. Tell them what document you need, and what relation you are to the person.

4. Look into a map book or atlas to see where the counties and towns are located.

5. Read local histories and local history of these places. You may want to inquire about the Historical Societies and the town or city historians there.

6. You may want to make a trip to visit the area your ancestors were from.

7. Try to get in touch with local libraries and genealogical societies before you plan a trip.

8. Keep a trip record of where and when you traveled, the places you visited, who you talked to, what you found.

9. Keep a record of costs incurred in doing research away from home.

RESEARCH AWAY FROM HOME

Locating Where Your Ancestors Came From

You can start with vital records, census indexes or other means to find out where your ancestors were born, married and died.

In The Handy Book, you can check in what town the county seat is, which is where the courthouse is located. Your ancestors might have lived in the same house and town, while the counties changed around them. So check the surrounding counties for records.

You can read the map books to see where the county or counties are. You can check if there are any local histories.

You can contact the county clerks in the areas where your ancestors lived, telling them what document you need and what relation you are to the person. Ask what the fee is and enclose a self-addressed stamped envelope for their reply. The fee is also noted in the booklet, "Where to Write for Vital Records."

You can ask the librarian at the reference desk to look up the libraries in that area, getting the address and phone numbers.

If you decide to take a trip, before you go, you may want to write or call the libraries and ask directions to get there, find out their hours and of the courthouse and other establishments. You could ask about the local genealogical society and if there is a town historian.

You can write to the local genealogical society and state what family you are looking for and ask if there are any records on them. Many societies keep records of all the town's early inhabitants or could tell you where to find the records.

Also, The Handy Book lists genealogical and historical societies, libraries, archives and publications for the whole state as well as what printed census schedules are availble.

Taking a Research Trip

After reading what you can about the history of the area where your ancestors lived, taking a trip there in person is very rewarding.

RESEARCH AWAY FROM HOME

All my husband's ancestors lived in other states than the one we lived in. All research had to be done by mail. But finally we were ready to take our first research trip. We were going to Illinois. I had no idea what to expect, so I wrote to the genealogical society in the town where my husband's great-grandfather was buried.

I got a nice reply from one of the members outlining where the cemetery was, the hours of the courthouse and some general information.

We were lucky as this gentleman met us at our motel and took us personally for two days to the cemetery, the courthouse, to the library in the next town where the records were. Then he introduced us to a genealogist who had many records in her library at home and had information nowhere else to be found.

Our guide was retired and had lived there all his life and was so knowledgeable. Everyone we met was so helpful. No one would take any money for their help, but suggested a donation to their genealogical society, which we did.

Later, we wrote to this gentleman asking him to look up records for us and he did so. He was 85 and we were very impressed with his energy and very appreciative of his help.

So, it is very helpful if, before you go, you write or call ahead to the library or genealogical society.

The Actual Visit

When you visit your ancestors' town, it's so exciting. You can see the roads they walked on, the countryside they saw; you can imagine how it looked in the early years when they first arrived.

You can look for a town historian and talk to him. At the local library, ask about the county histories and family genealogies. Search the old newspapers there for obituaries and articles about your family.

Ask if they have any old copies at the newspaper office. Sometimes, we found when the new publisher took over, the old copies were thrown away, which was very disappointing to us.

Go to the courthouse and, through deeds, see if you can find the land on which they lived. Perhaps the house is still standing. Perhaps one of your relatives is still living there.

Visit the cemeteries, see the town square, observe the main street. Your ancestors must have shopped there. Some main streets have been there since the turn of the century and haven't changed that much, maybe a few different stores.

We found a Civil War monument in the town square and my husband's ancestor's name was engraved on it, along with the names of several of his brothers who fought for the Union.

We even found a hundred-year old gentleman in a one-hundred year hotel who remembered, as a child, seeing my husband's great-grandfather and his brothers working in their shoe shop on Main Street.

Note Taking on Trips

Every trip we took for research, I wrote in my notebook about when we arrived, how we went first to the courthouse, and what we found there.

Then I wrote which library we visited, its address, hours, telephone number, who we talked to (in case we wanted to call and inquire about some material we had seen or missed), and what we found.

If we visited cemeteries, I wrote how we found them, who we talked to, how to get in the cemetery, where the grave was in relation to the entrance, if there was a family plot.

When we found the grave or graves, I drew up a plan on where the tombstone or tombstones were in relation to each other, the street the gravesite was on, plus any extra items, like a Civil War cross. The carvings on the tombstone are important and symbolic, so I copied them on my paper. I also photographed the site.

If we stayed 2 or 3 days as we usually did, every night I would write everything we did. I keep these notes in a separate folder. Many times I have to refer to the "Notes of a visit to Mt. Carroll, Illinois" or "Notes on a visit to the Maryland Archives."

To Sum Up:

1. If your ancestors were from another area, discover the counties and states your ancestors lived in. You may find this from vital record indexes, census indexes or other means.

2. Some counties were formed from other counties, so check The Handy Book where the neighboring county seats are.

3. Go to or write to the county clerks in the states where your ancestors lived.

4. Read local histories and local history of the area where your ancestors were located. See where it was in a map book or atlas.

5. You may want to make a trip to visit the town where your ancestors lived. Try to get in touch with local libraries and genealogical societies. Ask about historical societies or the town historian.

6. Keep a trip record of where and when you traveled, the places you visited, who you talked to, what you found.

7. Keep a record of cost of documents, postage, paper and copying, genealogical books and supplies purchased, cost of joining genealogical societies, and cost of travel in your research away from home.

CHAPTER 12

MY SEARCH

I'm only mentioning my search because there might be something helpful there as you begin your search.

I started with trying to find out where my husband's grandfather, Harvey Dunster Fisher, was buried.

Many years ago, my husband's mother and father had come to Columbus, Ohio, where we lived, saying they had finally found Harvey's grave. Harvey was a minister and a circuit rider in the Upper Peninsula of Michigan in the late 1800's. All we knew was that he was buried in Iron Mountain, Michigan, and they had bought him a new gravestone. We never thought to ask them anything about it, but 30 years later we decided to go find the grave.

I wrote the county clerk in Dickenson County in the Upper Peninsula of Michigan. I found the county by checking at the reference desk of the library and they looked it up for me. Later, I bought the Handy Book, which had that information.

The county clerk referred me to the sexton of the cemetary, who referred me to a lady who had compiled a log of information for the Dickenson County Genealogical Society.

Sometimes, I think it is helpful to write directly to the genealogical society, the town historian or historical society. However, sometimes they write back they don't have anyone who is able to look up anything for you; other times, they look up information on your ancestor and send it to you, as well as tell you hours in their library and other places you can visit or write to. It depends on how busy they are.

I found out that after all my work, my library might have had some of this information in their genealogy room. So it is good to check out what you can find locally before you write.

MY SEARCH

We heard from the kind lady who had rubbed tracings of my husband's grandfather's grave; she sent us a copy of the death obituary which was in the town records. She mentioned a person in Wisconsin who was keeping clippings on the town of Florence, Wisconsin, and might have information about the grandfather. We wrote to him and discovered the grandfather, Harvey, was buried on his lot. We also found there was another Harvey Fisher in Florence who had also died and we had to sort out their clippings.

I must say that much of my information was received from talking to people and being referred to other people that I would never have dreamed would have so much information on my husband's relatives.

We drove to Iron Mountain to see for ourselves the grave and search newspaper clippings in the genealogical room of the library. This was our first research trip.

We were fortunate because we found a man in the township hall who knew where the grave was and the librarian was helpful in locating clippings from July 1898 to January 1899 about Rev. Harvey Dunster Fisher--how helpful he was as pastor of the Peoples Church and how he died from pneumonia at age 40 in 1899. We searched for his church, but found it had burned down in 1957 with all the records.

We found out he was buried on someone's else's lot because the family didn't have the money to bury him and that gentleman donated them his lot. There were hard times that winter.

No one in my husband's family knew what Harvey's mother and father's names were, but the death certificate we obtained for him at the courthouse listed as his father Elhanan Fisher from Pennsylvania, but no county or years. It did say Harvey was born in Mt. Carroll, Carroll County, Illinois.

I wrote to the Mt. Carroll Genealogical Society, the address for which I found in the Handy Book. We drove there and found records and graves, helped by a member of the Society. Because of this information, we were able to work back to Chester County, Pennsylvania, to 1749.

This is how I started my genealogical search.

CHAPTER 13

GETTING IT ALL TOGETHER

1. Keep your records current by keeping a running tab on all you do, so you don't have to do things over. Write a running summary or history of each ancestor you are working on. Review the individual summaries and histories.

2. Each time you work on your genealogy, stop and enter all the data you obtained. List your ideas together for easy reference.

3. Don't let your notes pile up over months. As often as possible, try to write them on one sheet or so; try to attend to some of them every week. Then--update. Throw out all those scraps of paper.

4. Keep your binders current: your main family binder, census records kept for each person by year, continuous correspondence log, diary of daily doings, orderings, library research, census film readings, etc.

5. It is very important not to stop your search. When one avenue fails, try another. Write to a historical society, another genealogical society, go to some workshops; try a new approach to a census finding--look for a different state or locate a different relative.

6. Stop occasionally to redefine your perspective. Go over your notes. Perhaps you missed a crucial clue. Leaf thru your reference books; perhaps something new will catch your eye you can follow up on.

7. And most important, verify, verify, verify every fact, every circumstance, every location, every relationship; analyze the evidence from sources; then, document each one very thoroughly so that anyone may go to each source and find exactly what you found.

GETTING IT ALL TOGETHER

Keeping Current

It is much easier to keep current in all phases of your research if you keep track of them all about the same time, entering the necessary items in each binder and log.

I did these things one at a time over a long period of time as I happened to think that this way would be an easier way to keep some records or I came across some other ideas. Then I had to go back and look up everything again, like, to update the correspondence log and copy all the census records to keep them in one book. If I had thought to do everything at the beginning, I would have saved immeasurable time.

If you are organized from the start, each new piece of information you uncover will have a place to fit into. And you will be developing the system most efficient for you.

As You Keep Searching

If you have come to a standstill in locating children or parents of some of your ancestors, consider the naming systems used long ago to give you a clue. Not every family used this system, but it is worth a try.

A Naming System or Pattern

The first son was named after the father's father, the first daughter after the mother's mother. The next son would be named after the wife's father, and the next daughter after the father's mother. The next son would be named after the father, the daughter after the mother. People from different countries and areas used variations of this naming pattern.

Another naming pattern, used in our family, is where the oldest son has his mother's maiden name as his middle name.

Try different methods to get a new viewpoint on your research.

A Little History

One way to keep current is every time you have gathered some information, write a little history of that person.

A GENEALOGICAL HISTORY

(Your ancestor) was born on _____ in_____. His

father was _____and his mother was _____. He

died on _____in_____(place)

from _____at age ___. He was buried at _____

on _____. His will was dated _____ and

proved on _____.

(Your ancestor) was married to _____on_____

in_____. His wife was born on _____

in_____. Her father was_____ and her

mother was_____. They were from _____. She

died on_____in_____. Her will was dated _____ and

proved_____.

(Your ancestor's) occupation was _____. He belonged

to the _____ church. If he was in the military,

his record is_____. His achievements in

life were: _____.

You may then tell about his life, travels, and events, such as births of children, moving to new homes, his occupations, church memberships and finally the end of his life.

A genealogical summary at the end could list all his children with pertinent information on each.

GETTING IT ALL TOGETHER

As noted earlier, you should check to see if you have established probability that, for example, your father was his father's son, by using various records and that you did the same for the preceding generations, linking each generation together. This will tie all generations back to the first ancestor found.

After you determine the main line of descendancy, you can go back and follow the siblings.

A Numbering System

When you reach the point that you start writing a summary for each person, you will want to number the generations and children as they descend.

At present, there are three numbering systems: the Register System, the Record System (a variation of the Register System) which I use, and the Henry System. You may want to look up all three in other material.

I found the easiest system for me was the Record or National Genealogical Society Quarterly System. Three types of numbers are used; one to identify the individual, one to indicate the generation he is in (in superscript), and one to show his place in the birth order of his family in small Roman numerals. Children who will be more fully detailed are shown with a $+$ at the left.

For example, in our family history, The Wristen/Riston Family, Number 1 was used for the earliest ancestor, the father of Elisha Riston. We continued with Number 2 for Elisha Riston, his son, 3, 4, etc. for Elisha's siblings.

By the time, we got to Elijah Wristen, son of Elisha Riston (he changed his name around 1800), he was number 17 from the first Riston, who was the father of Elisha. Elijah was the 7th child of Elisha, so vii was used.

Elijah was in the third generation, so ^{3} was used. The $+$ shows more information on him will follow. In parenthesis was his father, Elisha, the second generation, with a ^{2} used. We didn't know Elisha's father's first name, so we left that blank, showing only that he was the first generation: ^{1}.

Below as an example is Elijah and two of his siblings:

+ 17. vii. Elijah^3 Riston (____-^{1}, Elisha^2) b. ca. 1807; d. ca. 1880; m. 1. Leona Sisk, 11 Oct 1832; 2. Nancy Davis, 1850; 3. Mary Skidmore, ca. 1865.

+ 18. viii. Reuben M. Riston, b. ca. 1810, d. ca, 1885; m. Vernetta Adkins (1813-1890), 9 Oct 1837.

19. ix. Mary (Polly) Riston, b. ca. 1813, d. unknown; m. Jesse Hardison, 2 Mar 1840. (Christian Co. KY, Mar. Book 1797-1850) No further information.

Where there is no further information, documentation is included in that person's listing. In the above, documentation for Elijah and Reuben was included in the text of the little history written for each of them.

A very good explanation and illustration of the numbering system is in the article "Numbering Your Genealogy: Sound and Simple Systems," by Joan Ferris Curran (National Genealogical Society Quarterly, Vol. 79, No. 3, September 1991).

As I went back in time, I felt as if these people were still alive and that I knew them. I could picture them going about their business. Then when I chanced across a photograph of some of them, old and grizzled and with long beards, I couldn't relate to them at all, since, for some reason, I pictured them young and vital, as I traced them from the beginning of their lives. But they were our ancestors and lived day-to-day lives just as we do.

To Sum Up

1. Keep records current. Keep up summaries of work done and histories of ancestors.

2 If you come to a stopping point in your research, try other angles to get a different viewpoint. Go back over your material looking for clues.

3. Your family genealogy should be coming together.

CHAPTER 14

SOME POINTS OF INTEREST FOR LATER ON

1. After you have your basic data, you will want to read more sophisticated how-to books and begin to do more advanced research.

2. When I finally found enough information, I finished typing up summaries of each generation. I didnt know exactly what to do next. I kept them a while and reread some of my material. Then I found the Chicago Manual of Style.

    A new revision had just come out (1993) and I bought a copy. It really opened my eyes on how a book format goes and I was able to retype my summaries properly in a relatively short time. So I suggest you see this volume at your library or bookstore when you are ready.

3. There will come a certain point when you realize you have to stop; tie this material together before it is all lost.

4. Something I didn't know: when you do complete a genealogy or family history, you may send two copies to the Library of Congress. They will give you a number for it. Send it to: the Library of Comgress, Exchange and Gifts Dept., 10 first St. SE, Washington, DC 20540 (1996).

5. Another thing I didn't know: what items were covered by copyright and couldn't be copied for publication. From the beginning, as you collect items, note if they are under copyright and permission has to be written for. Where to write is usually at the front of the publication.

6. You may also want to prepare a medical family tree, using all your documents and family information, of your ancestors' onsets of illnesses and causes of death to establish a pattern of genetic inheritance.

CONCLUSION

What Genealogy Means To Me

Preparing a genealogy means getting down all you know. Then, adding what you find out about your family. So, later, your children don't have to wonder, "what was my grandmother's maiden name? What was my great grandfather's first name?"

Genealogy means to me that your descendants are left with some idea of where their people came from, what they were like, all those lives stretching back behind all of us.

Genealogy also means to me that we share our information, sending it to library genealogy rooms in the states our ancestors came from, especially when nothing could be found about them there; and sharing it with all the researchers who gave us their research. And sharing it with our family.

Documentation

Documentation is the most important facet of genealogical research. Nothing is more frustrating than an undocumented family genealogy. Many people perpetuate unproven data, which then takes so much time to verify. Always state if there is a doubt or you can't find a source or if there are conflicts in dates or data. Other researchers will then know what to pursue.

The Family Historian

You must think, "Who is our family historian?" If there is no one, it would be nice if you took on these duties and then found someone to pass them down to.

The Depth of Genealogical Research

It's hard to believe how much more is involved in genealogical research, to what depth it goes. The basics just skim the surface; I had no idea of how much more there was until I went on. Every day I come across deeper and more involved methods and avenues of research. So there's no end of ways to solve the problem; it's just a matter of unearthing them.

What Should You Do Next

I tried to cover the basics--the rest, burned records, more involved land records, searches for military records, migration, lost women, and many other topics, you'll have to read about in regular How-To books and go to genealogical seminars to learn about.

There is a huge amount of reference material available. You just have to find it.

Someday

It's not too soon to be thinking of the day you will start writing your genealogy, incorporating all your material with your documentation up-to-date, your numbering in order, with the front matter (title page, preface, introduction, tables of contents and illustrations) and back matter (appendixes, bibliography, index) ready to write.

Even though you are just starting, if you keep a goal in sight, it will be easier to arrange your material in generations or in chapters as you go along, adding to it, and changing it to make it clearer. It's easier to do this from the very beginning than to wait till you have a mountain of paper and wonder how to go about starting putting it in order.

As you are doing this, think how you'll write your preface--explaining how you started doing your genealogy, explaining all the steps you took, where you found your information, the methods you used to organize it and format it, explaining why you did it. It's more pleasant to do this as you go.

Why Keep Track of the Cost?

At the beginning is the time to start keeping a running total of expenses or the cost of getting this material together.

Later, if you arrange to have your book printed or do it yourself, like I did, you will want to show what your expenses were for research as well as printing, binding, and advertising. If eventually you decide to make a printer-ready copy and arrange to have it printed, acting as the publisher, you can deduct some of the expenses when you start selling some of your books.

Though that may be in the future, now is the time to give it some thought.

Your Final Goal

Think about your final goal from the beginning and all the little goals along the way and you'll be making your way step-by-step to compiling your family history.

And To Sum It All Up

The bottom line is that you can only learn by getting in there and doing it yourself.

BIBLIOGRAPHY

Barnes, Donald R. and Lackey, Richard S. Write It Right. 2nd ed. Ocala, FL: Lyon Press, 1988.

The Chicago Manual of Style. 14th ed. Chicago: University of Chicago Press, 1993.

Cerny, Johni and Wendy Elliott. The Library: A Guide to the LDS Family History Library. Salt Lake City: Ancestry, 1988.

Curran, Joan Ferris. "Numbering Your Genealogy: Sound and Simple Systems." National Genealogical Society Quarterly Vol. 79, No. 3 (September 1991): 183-193.

Doane, Gilbert H. Searching for Your Ancestors. 4th ed. Minneapolis, MN: University of Minnesota Press, 1973.

Drake, Paul, J.D. In Search of Family History: A Starting Place. Bowie: Heritage Books, 1992.

Eakle, Arlene and Johni Cerny, eds. The Source: A Guidebook of American Genealogy. Salt Lake City: Ancestry Publishing Co., 1984.

Filby, P. William. A Bibliography of American County Histories. Balt: Genealogical Pub. Co., 1985.

Genealogy Bulletin. Bountiful, Utah: The AGLL Genealogical Services.

Genealogical Helper. Logan, UT: Everton Publishers, Inc.

Greenwood, Val D. The Researcher's Guide to American Genealogy. 2nd ed. Balt.: Genealogical Publishing Co., 1990.

Guide to Genealogical Research in the Archives. Washington, D.C.: National Archives Trust Fund Board, 1985.

The Handy Book for Genealogists. Logan, UT: Everton Publishers, 1991.

Heritage Quest. Bountiful, Utah: The AGLL Genealogical Services.

Hinshaw, William Wade, ed. Encyclopedia of American Quaker Genealogy. 6 vols. 1936. Rpt., Balt.: Gen. Pub. Co. 1969.

Lackey, Richard S. Cite Your Sources. Jackson, MS: University Press of Mississippi, 1980.

PERiodical Source Index (PERSI). Fort Wayne, Ind: Allen County Public Library Foundation, 1997. (It is now available (1998) on CD-ROM from Ancestry, Inc. PO Box 990, Orem UT 84059)

Schreiner-Yantis, Netti, ed. Genealogical and Local History Books in Print. 4th ed. 3 vols. Springfield, Va., 1985.

Where to Write for Birth, Marriage, Divorce and Death Records. U.S. Department of Health and Human Services (Superintendent of Documents, Washington, D.C.: U.S. Government Printing Office, 1993.)

www.ingramcontent.com/pod-product-compliance
Lightning Source LLC
Chambersburg PA
CBHW080335270326
41927CB00014B/3239